Charles Taylor

The Oxyrhynchus logia and the apocryphal gospels

Charles Taylor

The Oxyrhynchus logia and the apocryphal gospels

ISBN/EAN: 9783337713836

Printed in Europe, USA, Canada, Australia, Japan

Cover: Foto ©Thomas Meinert / pixelio.de

More available books at **www.hansebooks.com**

THE
OXYRHYNCHUS LOGIA

AND THE

APOCRYPHAL GOSPELS

BY THE

REV. CHARLES TAYLOR, D.D.

MASTER OF ST. JOHN'S COLLEGE, CAMBRIDGE

Oxford

AT THE CLARENDON PRESS

MDCCCXCIX

Oxford
PRINTED AT THE CLARENDON PRESS
BY HORACE HART, M.A.
PRINTER TO THE UNIVERSITY

PREFACE

A LEAFLET of papyrus, found on the site of Oxyrhynchus, in Egypt, in the winter of 1896-7, contains the few short Greek sayings which are the subject of this essay. Their discoverers and first editors, the two Oxford scholars Mr. Grenfell and Mr. Hunt, called them in the same language *Logia*, that is *oracles* (Rom. iii. 2), of JESUS.

The fragment has the appearance of having belonged to a small manual, containing sayings detached from their contexts in some larger and more costly Codex or Codices and fitted compactly together by a compiler, who changed a word here and there, and prefixed the formula of citation *Saith Jesus* to successive paragraphs.

The compositeness of the Logiographer's sections is well illustrated by Logion VII, on the city that 'can neither fall nor be hid,' which blends the saying, 'A city set on a hill cannot be hid,' with the parable of the house which 'fell not; for it was founded upon the rock.' Others of the Logia, likewise duplex, which cannot be traced back to the New Testament, may have been derived from one or from more than one of the lost documents of Christian antiquity, such as the Gospel according to the Egyptians, which some suppose to have contained all the sayings on the papyrus.

The latter part of the essay touches upon some things in the Apocryphal Gospels, considered in themselves or in relation to the Oxyrhynchus Logia. In particular it is pointed out that there are seeming traces of the remarkable Logion V in the Gospel of Thomas, a Gospel of the Infancy, to which the writer's attention was first attracted through some acute criticisms by Dr. J. M. Cotterill in his *Peregrinus Proteus* (1879).

Use has been made of Messrs. Grenfell and Hunt's two editions of the text of the Logia; of Professors Lock and Sanday's *Two Lectures* upon them and the works named therein; and of other published dissertations or notes bearing upon the subject, which will be referred to in due course. For valuable suggestions privately communicated I am indebted to Dr. Gifford, Dr. E. A. Abbott, Dr. Rendel Harris, and Professor Bywater.

The essay is founded upon a lecture given in Oxford, at Mansfield College, in the Easter Term of 1898.

C. TAYLOR.

CAMBRIDGE,
March 25, 1899.

CONTENTS

	PAGE
THE OXYRHYNCHUS LOGIA .	3
THE APOCRYPHAL GOSPELS .	85

THE
OXYRHYNCHUS LOGIA

THE OXYRHYNCHUS LOGIA

I

INTRODUCTION.

ON the right bank of the Nile, some forty leagues south of Cairo, stands 'Abu Girgeh.' 'A ride of seven miles N.E. from Abu Girgeh brings the traveller to the wretched Arab town of Behnesa, which occupies the site of Oxyrhynchus. The Greek name of the city reveals its antiquity. It was so called, as Strabo tells us (xvii. p. 812 τιμῶσι δὲ τὸν ὀξύρρυγχον), from the worship of a Nile fish of the sturgeon class, *with pointed head.*'

So writes Professor Swete in his Lecture on 'The Oxyrhynchus Fragment,' published in the *Expository Times* of September, 1897; and he adds that Ruffinus describes Oxyrhynchus in glowing terms, telling us that it had a population of ten thousand monks and twenty thousand virgins[*], and that there was not a pagan or a heretic to be found in it. 'This was perhaps in the last years of the fourth century. But the history of Oxyrhynchus as a Christian city goes further back. A bishop of Oxyrhynchus signed the Seleucian Creed of 359, and other bishops preceded him in the see. There is no reason to doubt that Christianity was already active in this nome and town in the third and even in the second century.'

[*] On these large numbers of monks and virgins see 'The Lausiac History of Palladius,' by Dom Cuthbert Butler, in the Cambridge *Texts and Studies*, vol. vi. no. 1, p. 201 (1898).

The fragment above mentioned was first edited by its discoverers, Mr. Bernard P. Grenfell and Mr. Arthur S. Hunt, for the Egyptian Exploration Fund, and printed at the Clarendon Press in 1897, under the double title,—

ΛΟΓΙΑ ΙΗϹΟΥ

SAYINGS OF OUR LORD.

The sayings are written on a single leaf of papyrus, from which something has been worn or torn off at the lower end ; and facsimiles of the *verso* and the *recto* are given in the first edition, which will be quoted as 'G. H.'

Later in the same year were published, in a tract of forty-nine pages, at the Clarendon Press, *Two Lectures on the 'Sayings of Jesus' recently discovered at Oxyrhynchus,* delivered at Oxford by Professors Lock and Sanday, preceded by a most useful Bibliography, with a condensed summary of previous criticisms. This work is hereinafter referred to by the abbreviation 'L. S.'

Dr. Edwin A. Abbott has written on *The Logia of Behnesa* in *The American Journal of Theology* for January, 1898, pp. 1–27.

The volume entitled *The Oxyrhynchus Papyri, Part I,* Clarendon Press, 1898, edited by Messrs. Grenfell and Hunt for the Egypt Exploration Fund, Graeco-Roman Branch, begins with the ΛΟΓΙΑ ΙΗϹΟΥ, of which a revised text is given, with some introductory remarks.

In the *editio princeps* (G. H.) it was said to be 'difficult to imagine a title better suited to a series of sayings, each introduced by the phrase λέγει Ἰησοῦς, than Logia.'

This defence of the Greek title ΛΟΓΙΑ ΙΗϹΟΥ, freely rendered 'Sayings of our Lord,' wants a word of explanation. The generality of sayings introduced by λέγει, *saith,* would not and could not be called *Logia,* i.e. oracles. But when Jesus spoke, it was 'as the oracles of God,' and His utterances might therefore be so called. 'From Herodotus downwards' *logion* has meant *oracle,* and it is translated by that word in the four places in which it is found in the New Testament, Acts vii. 38 ; Rom. iii. 2 ; Heb. v. 12 ; 1 Pet. iv. 11.

Introduction 5

We must not inadvertently assume that the sayings for which Messrs. Grenfell and Hunt have invented a deservedly popular Greek title, meaning *Oracles of Jesus*, are some of the original ' Logia ' written by the Evangelist St. Matthew, who, according to a statement of Papias of Hierapolis in the course of his own expositions of the Oracles of the Lord, wrote *The Oracles* in the Hebrew tongue (Swete, p. 545 ; L. S. pp. 16, 29). But the Oxyrhynchus sayings in question are now known everywhere by the name 'The Logia.' As a short, distinctive, practical title, we shall accordingly use it without further remark ; and we shall call their compiler the Logiographer.

In *The Oxyrhynchus Papyri* (p. 3) the contents of the fragment are grouped and rendered as follows, the clause in brackets being merely a conjectural addition :—

Logion I, *verso* 1-4. '. . . and then shalt thou see clearly to cast out the mote that is in thy brother's eye.'

Logion II, 4-11. 'Jesus saith, Except ye fast to the world, ye shall in no wise find the kingdom of God ; and except ye make the sabbath a real sabbath, ye shall not see the Father.'

Logion III, 11-21. 'Jesus saith, I stood in the midst of the world and in the flesh was I seen of them, and I found all men drunken, and none found I athirst among them, and my soul grieveth over the sons of men, because they are blind in their heart, and see not . . .'

Logion IV, *recto* 1. '. . . poverty.'

Logion V, 2-9. 'Jesus saith, Wherever there are two, they are not without God, and wherever there is one alone, I say, I am with him. Raise the stone, and there thou shalt find Me, cleave the wood and there am I.'

Logion VI, 9-14. 'Jesus saith, A prophet is not acceptable in his own country, neither doth a physician work cures upon them that know him.'

Logion VII, 15-20. 'Jesus saith, A city built upon the top of a high hill and stablished, can neither fall nor be hid.'

Logion VIII, 20-22. 'Jesus saith, Thou hearest with one ear (but the other ear thou hast closed).'

We shall treat of the sayings in these eight 'Logia' as belonging to seven sections, the fourth comprising Logion III and Logion IV. The introductory formula, 'Jesus saith,' is discussed under Logion II.

II

LOGION I.

] καὶ τότε διαβλέψεις ἐκβαλεῖν τὸ κάρφος τὸ ἐν τῷ ὀφθαλμῷ τοῦ ἀδελφοῦ σου.

... and then shalt thou see clearly to cast out the mote that is in thy brother's eye.

This end of a saying, with which the *verso* or first page of the papyrus (L. S. p. 38) commences, is identical with the last clause of St. Luke vi. 42 according to the Received Text and the English Authorized and Revised Versions. But Westcott and Hort's text of the Greek Testament, in agreement with Codex B and some other manuscripts, gives the inverted order of words, 'and then shalt thou see clearly *the mote that is in thy brother's eye to cast out.*' Thus the Logion would differ somewhat from St. Luke's form of the saying. It differs also from St. Matthew's, '... and then shalt thou see clearly to cast out the mote *out of* thy brother's eye.'

But in St. Matt. vii. 3-5 we read, 'And why beholdest thou *the mote that is in thy brother's eye*, but considerest not the beam that is in thine own eye? Or how wilt thou say to thy brother, Let me pull out the mote out of thine eye; and, behold, a beam is in thine own eye? Thou hypocrite, first cast out the beam out of thine own eye; *and then shalt thou see clearly to cast out* the mote out of thy brother's eye.' Here the words italicized in verses 5 and

3 together make up the extant part of the Logion, which might accordingly have been derived from St. Matthew's Gospel as it has come down to us, quite as simply as from St. Luke's with the readings of Westcott and Hort. When only such slight differences have to be weighed in the balance, we cannot say that the Logion agrees more with the one Gospel than with the other until we know the exact words of the Evangelists. The collation of it with the Canonical Gospels raises the difficult question, To what degree of approximation can we rely upon any modern critical edition of the New Testament?

There are those who regard Westcott and Hort's text as not 'neutral,' but Egyptian. Thus Dr. Salmon writes in *Some Thoughts on the Textual Criticism of the New Testament:* 'To sum up in conclusion, I have but to repeat my belief that what Westcott and Hort have restored is the text which had the highest authority in Alexandria in the third century, and may have reached that city in the preceding one.' An early Egyptian text would have special value as a standard by which to test a contemporary Oxyrhynchus document.

III

LOGION II.

Λέγει Ἰησοῦς,

(A) Ἐὰν μὴ νηστεύσητε τὸν κόσμον οὐ μὴ εὕρητε τὴν βασιλείαν τοῦ θεοῦ *.

Καί,

(B) Ἐὰν μὴ σαββατίσητε τὸ σάββατον οὐκ ὄψεσθε τὸν πατέρα.

Saith Jesus,

Except ye fast the world, ye shall in no wise find the kingdom of God.

And,

Except ye sabbatize the sabbath, ye shall not see the Father.

* On a proposed new reading instead of θεοῦ, see *Conclusion.*

Logion II has been thought to consist of a single saying introduced by the formula of citation, 'Saith Jesus.' But probably it was made up of two separate sayings, *Except ye fast &c.*, and *Except ye sabbatize &c.*, put together on account of their affinity and parallelism, and connected by an editorial 'And.' The use of this conjunction as a short formula of citation, meaning 'And *he saith*,' is well established; and examples of it are given below from the New Testament and Pirké Aboth. Others may be found in Resch's *Agrapha* and elsewhere. In Professor Bywater's *Heracliti Ephesii Reliquiae* (Oxon. 1877) sayings of Heraclitus are introduced one after another with καὶ ὅτι in the passage quoted from M. Antoninus iv. 46 in the footnote on Fragment V (p. 3).

(1) HEB. i. 5-10.

5 For unto which of the angels said he at any time,
    Thou art my Son,
    This day have I begotten thee?
and again,
    I will be to him a Father,
    And he shall be to me a Son?
7 And of the angels he saith,
    Who maketh his angels winds,
    And his ministers a flame of fire:
8 but of the Son *he saith*,
    Thy throne, O God, is for ever and ever;
    And the sceptre of uprightness is the sceptre of thy
      kingdom.
9   Thou hast loved righteousness, and hated iniquity;
    Therefore God, thy God, hath anointed thee
    With the oil of gladness above thy fellows.
10 And,
    Thou, Lord, in the beginning hast laid the founda-
      tion of the earth,
    And the heavens are the works of thy hands.

Here in verse 10 a simple 'And,' in the sense 'And *he*

Logion II   9

saith,' marks the transition from Psalm xlv to Psalm cii. In Westcott and Hort's Greek Testament the καί at the beginning of verse 10 not only has a line to itself, but is printed in different type from the quotations between which it stands.

(2) PIRKÉ ABOTH.

This Tract supplies numerous instances of sayings in Hebrew linked together by VAU, *and*, beginning at the beginning with the men of the Great Synagogue, who '*said* three things, Be deliberate in judgment ; *and* Raise up many disciples; *and* Make a fence to the law.'

Pirké Aboth, in Hebrew and English, is contained in the Authorized Jewish Prayer Book as edited by Mr. S. Singer, where in chap. ii of the Tract we read in the translation, 'Hillel said, Separate not thyself from the congregation ; trust not in thyself until the day of thy death ; judge not thy neighbour until thou art come into his place ; and say not anything which cannot be understood at once, in the hope that it will be understood in the end ; neither say, When I have leisure I will study ; perchance thou wilt not have leisure.'

With a more literal translation of the Hebrew on the opposite page of the Prayer Book the paragraph would run, 'Hillel *said*, Separate not from ... *and* Trust not in thyself ... *and* Judge not thy neighbour ... *and* Say not anything ... *and* Say not, When I have leisure &c.' Thus we have five distinct sayings attributed to Hillel, the first introduced by *said* and the others by editorial *and* ... *and* ... *and* ... *and*.

In the same chapter it is recorded that Rabban Jochanan had five disciples, each of whom said three things; and the sayings of each of the five are connected by editorial *and*.

The 'And' in Logion II may in accordance with these analogies be a short formula of citation, and not part of a saying attributed to our Lord by the Logiographer.

We conclude that it is actually a word of the compiler, because (A) and (B) are apparently distinct sayings, and each is obviously complete without the other. We shall accordingly discuss them first separately and afterwards in relation to one another.

(A)

Ἐὰν μὴ νηστεύσητε τὸν κόσμον οὐ μὴ εὕρητε τὴν βασιλείαν τοῦ θεοῦ.

The construction 'Except ye fast *the world*' being new and strange, there are three courses open to us.

1.

We may accept the reading τὸν κόσμον as accurate and true, and render the saying, 'Except ye fast to the world &c.,' inserting a preposition in the English as our Versions do for example in the Beatitude, 'Blessed are they that hunger and thirst *righteousness*' (Matt. v. 6). Or we may make the accusative after 'fast' temporal, as in the *Didaché* chap. viii : 'And let your fasts not be with the hypocrites ; for they fast on Monday and Thursday (δευτέρᾳ σαββάτων καὶ πέμπτῃ), but ye shall fast τετράδα καὶ παρασκευήν, *during Wednesday and Friday*.' 'The fast which the Lord prescribes is world-long' (Swete, p. 546). 'His disciples were not to fast merely on Mondays and Thursdays, as the Pharisees did, but, so to speak, *all through worldly time*' (Abbott, p. 8). For other explanations of τὸν κόσμον, and for emendations of the saying (A), see L. S. p. 19.

2.

We may question the accuracy of τὸν κόσμον as a reading of what is in the manuscript. Its first decipherment was difficult owing in a measure to the strangeness of the result, for it was said, 'If the reading κόσμον is correct—and there seems to be no alternative—such an accusative after νηστεύειν, "fast to the world," is very harsh' (G. H.). But 'die βασιλεία schützt den κόσμος,' as Harnack well remarks. We therefore retain 'the world' as a natural antithesis to 'the kingdom of God.' The question remains, Did the scribe write TON KOCMON or TOY KOCMOY? To some who allow that he wrote KOCMON 'the reading of the article seems ambiguous' (L. S. p. 19). In the facsimile as it appears to me we have without doubt the accusative TON. The first stroke of the *nu* has indeed all but vanished, but the two strokes which follow are obviously the middle and last of a N.

3.

Granted that the scribe wrote τὸν κόσμον, this may be a clerical error for τοῦ κόσμου. In Clem. Alex. *Strom*. iii. 15 we find οἱ τοῦ κόσμου νηστεύοντες, *they that fast from the world*, 'not simply νηστεύοντες, but οἱ νηστεύοντες, as though they were a well-known class' (L. S. p. 19), where the writer not improbably rests upon the same authority as the Logiographer for his phrase νηστεύειν τοῦ κόσμου. If this passage of the *Stromateis* had stood alone as an authority for the phrase in question, it might have been conjectured that τοῦ κόσμου in it was possibly a corruption of τὸν κόσμον. But St. Clement writes also τῶν κοσμικῶν νηστεύειν (L. S. p. 9). Fasting (he says) is abstinence from food, and foodlessness connotes death. So spiritually we should *fast from worldly things* that we may die to the world.

To *fast from* is also expressed in two words by νηστεύειν ἀπό, a construction which may have been used in the Greek and the original Hebrew of Ecclus. xxxiv. 25–26.

In the Revised Version the passage runs thus:—
25 He that washeth himself *after touching* a dead body,
  and toucheth it again,
 What profit hath he in his washing?
26 Even so a man fasting *for* his sins;
  And going again, and doing the same;
 Who will listen to his prayer?
 And what profit hath he in his humiliation?

Instead of *after touching* (ver. 25) and instead of *for* (ver. 26), the Syriac, which may very well be an exact rendering of the original Hebrew, has the preposition ܡܢ, *from*. The Greek translator may accordingly have written ἀπό in both places, although the Greek Version now has ἀπό in the former place only and ἐπί in the latter before ἁμαρτιῶν. 'Fasting for his sins would be ἐπὶ ταῖς ἁμαρτίαις αὐτοῦ, and fasting ἐπὶ τῶν ἁμαρτιῶν αὐτοῦ would mean fasting in his sins, that is, continuing to sin while fasting, as in Isaiah lviii' (E. H. G.). Clearly this does not suit the context. But read ἀπό for ἐπί before ἁμαρτιῶν, and we get the required antithesis,

οὕτως ἄνθρωπος νηστεύων ἀπὸ τῶν ἁμαρτιῶν αὐτοῦ,
καὶ πάλιν πορευόμενος καὶ τὰ αὐτὰ ποιῶν.

The construction νηστεύειν ἀπό is used in Clem. *Strom.* vii. 12 (L. S. p. 9), where it is said of the true Christian that he fasts according to the law *from* base actions, and according to the perfection of the Gospel *from* evil thoughts. Briefly, he fasts from all sin; or in the language of the Logion he fasts from 'the world.' St. Clement, who quotes Ecclesiasticus, would have found there, according to our hypothesis, the construction νηστεύειν ἀπό.

In connexion with Logion II (A) Messrs. Grenfell and Hunt have aptly quoted Gal. vi. 14, 'by whom the world is *crucified* to me, and I unto the world.' Compare the saying of Jesus in Dr. Carl Schmidt's edition of *Das erste Buch Jeû*, published in vol. viii of *Texte und Untersuchungen* (1892), to the effect that, 'Blessed is he who has crucified the world, and not the world him,' 'Jesus, der Lebendige, antwortete und sprach zu seinen Aposteln, Selig ist der, welcher die Welt gekreuzigt hat und nicht die Welt hat ihn kreuzigen lassen.'

The Logion expresses the like in terms of fasting. We must renounce the world that we may attain to the kingdom of God. According as we read with the scribe τὸν κόσμον, or with St. Clement τοῦ κόσμου, we may render the saying, 'Except ye fast *to* (or *from*) the world, ye shall in no wise find the kingdom of God.' The reading τὸν κόσμον

Logion II

has found able advocates and interpreters. Nevertheless the simplest and best view seems to us to be that the scribe ought to have written,

ЄAN MH NHCTЄYCHTЄ TOY KOCMOY.

(B)

Ἐὰν μὴ σαββατίσητε τὸ σάββατον οὐκ ὄψεσθε τὸν πατέρα.

'Except ye *keep the sabbath*, ye shall not see the Father' (G. H.). Such is the natural English rendering of the saying; but in the Greek the word for 'keep' is *sabbatize*. Is the sabbath-keeping spoken of 'to be understood literally or metaphorically'? (L. S. p. 20). It has been said, on the one hand, that *sabbatize the sabbath* is the ordinary phrase in the Septuagint for observing the sabbath, references being given to Lev. xxiii. 32 and 2 Chron. xxvi. 21; and on the other hand that the phrase is nowhere to be found in that Version. The one statement is obviously inexact. On the other, which has been defended as true in the sense that 'sabbatize *the* sabbath,' with the article, is a phrase not used in the Septuagint, see below under Lev. xxiii. 32.

Turning to Hatch and Redpath's *Concordance* to the Greek Versions of the Old Testament, we find that the word *sabbatize* is used in the following places:—

1.

Exod. xvi. 30: So the people *rested* on the seventh day, LXX ἐσαββάτισεν ὁ λαὸς τῇ ἡμέρᾳ τῇ ἑβδόμῃ.

2 Macc. vi. 6: And a man could neither *keep the sabbath*, nor observe the feasts of the fathers, nor so much as confess himself to be a Jew.

2.

Lev. xxiii. 32 (A.V.): It shall be unto you a sabbath of rest, and ye shall afflict your souls: in the ninth day of the month at even, from even unto even, shall ye *celebrate* (marg. *rest*) your *sabbath*, Heb. שַׁבַּתְּכֶם תִּשְׁבְּתוּ, LXX σαββατιεῖτε τὰ σάββατα ὑμῶν. The Greek for 'a sabbath of rest' is σάββατα σαββάτων. On the plural σάββατα for a sabbath see Thayer, *N. T. Lex.* Σάββατα, in this verse, being plural in form only, we have virtually in the LXX, and we may suppose that some Version perhaps actually read, σαββατιεῖτε τὸ σάββατον ὑμῶν, with τὸ σάββατον following a part of σαββατίζειν.

3.

Lev. xxv. 2 : When ye come into the land which I give you, then shall the land *keep* (marg. *rest*) *a sabbath* unto the Lord. Aquila, σαββατιεῖ ἡ γῆ σάββατον.

Lev. xxvi. 34-35 (R.V.): Then shall the land enjoy her sabbaths, as long as it lieth desolate, and ye be in your enemies' land; even then shall the land rest, and enjoy her sabbaths. As long as it lieth desolate it shall have rest; even the rest which it had not in your sabbaths, when ye dwelt upon it, LXX τότε σαββατιεῖ ἡ γῆ . . . σαββατιεῖ ἃ οὐκ ἐσαββάτισεν ἐν τοῖς σαββάτοις ὑμῶν.

2 Chron. xxxvi. 21 *a*: To fulfil the word of the Lord by the mouth of Jeremiah, until the land had enjoyed her sabbaths, LXX τὰ σάββατα αὐτῆς σαββατίσαι. In 21 *b* and again in 1 Esdras i. 55 (58) σαββατίζειν is used without σάββατα of the land's keeping sabbath.

Thus *sabbatize* is used in three ways. (1) By itself and without *sabbath* it means to keep sabbath in the ordinary sense, i.e. to observe the seventh day of the week as a day of rest. (2) Followed by *sabbath* it means in a verse of Leviticus to keep the Day of Atonement. (3) With or without *sabbath* it is used of the observance of the sabbatical year. In no case does to 'sabbatize a sabbath' mean to keep the sabbath in the ordinary sense.

The saying (B), we conclude, inculcates something altogether different from keeping the Jewish Sabbath in the Jewish way; the stress being on the *sabbatizing* rather than on the *sabbath*, i.e. on the manner rather than on the occasion of the observance. To keep the true sabbath truly is to desist from sin (L. S. p. 20), and such day so kept is a Sabbath 'of the Lord' or Lord's Day. The saying has been abundantly illustrated by a number of well-known passages from early patristic writings, the authors of which may have been acquainted with some form of it, if not with the compilation of the Logiographer. Some of them 'spiritualize both fasting and Sabbath-keeping in one and the same context' (L. S. p. 20), at the same time quoting the Old Testament, on which the Logion rests, as we shall endeavour to shew in the following notes on its component parts in relation to one another.

(A) and (B)

The following is a Jewish view of the Logion :—

The second of the recently published Logia has exercised the minds of the learned, partly because they could not detect the connexion between its two component parts: the Fast and the Sabbath. Yet when it is borne in mind that in Jesus' time the Sabbath mentioned in Lev. xxiii. 27 was the "Great Fast," צומא רבא, it will at once become manifest that that verse, which the Editors and others only quote as a witness for the idiom of "sabbatizing the Sabbath" (a literal translation of the Hebrew original, and for this reason peculiar only to the LXX), forms the basis for both parts of the Logion, inasmuch as in Jesus' time the self-affliction enjoined there was universally understood to mean Fasting. There can hardly be a doubt that Jesus, in common with the Pharisaic rabbis, urged the spiritual celebration of that solemn day in both its aspects of Fast and Sabbath, in accordance with the Prophets of old, see e.g. Isa. i. 13, for the proper Sabbath; Zech. vii, viii, as to fasting; Isa. lviii as to both together; the latter prophecy was probably pronounced on the "Great Fast," as it is still read on that day in the Synagogue. The close parallelism which is thus found to exist between the two clauses explains also sufficiently the Accusative Case in τὸν κόσμον (=τὸ σάββατον), which was the other perplexing thing in the Logion.'

This suggestive critique of the second Logion was contributed by Dr. M. Berlin to the *Jewish Quarterly Review* for October, 1897, a footnote on the word 'rabbis' supplying references to the last *mishnah* of Joma and the first of Taanith II with the Gemara upon it.

In the same number of the *Jewish Quarterly Review* Mr. Joseph Jacobs, in a notice of Harnack, *Ueber die jüngst entdeckten Sprüche Jesu*, wrote on the second Saying:—

'At first sight this saying has a strong Judaizing tendency. The emphasis laid upon the Sabbath and upon fasting as prerequisites of salvation might come from any contemporary Rabbi. But closer inspection shows that the saying has rather an anti-Jewish tendency, for it is "fasting to the *world*" that is enjoined, not physical fasting; so, too, according to the parallelism of Hebrew writing and *thinking*, the observance of the Sabbath must also have a spiritual sense here . . . the somewhat peculiar Greek form used, σαββατίσητε τὸ σάββατον, indicates a derivative meaning which directly connects it with the Great Fast, for there can be little doubt that it is a literal translation of the Hebrew, שבתו שבתכם, used in Leviticus xxiii. 32 with reference to the Day of Atonement. . . . the reference to the world and to the Father serves to show that this saying represents the views of the second or third generation of the Church rather than of its founder. In particular the reference to the Father seems rather to come from the circle of ideas in which the fourth Gospel grew.'

Dr. K. Kohler again, in *The American Hebrew* (Dec. 10, 1897), founds the saying (B) upon Lev. xxiii. 32, and he continues: 'Now our saintly preacher surely thinks of the famous chapter in Isaiah lviii, read in the synagogue on the great Fast Day, which holds out the promise of "delight in the Lord" to those that fast INWARDLY, not for outward appearance . . . and make your Sabbath of Sabbaths a day of spiritual elevation; then you will see the Redemption. This was exactly the tradition of the Rabbinical saints: "If Israel will only observe two Sabbaths successively in reality, the Redemption is sure to come" (Sabbath 118 b).'

The *haftarah* or Lesson from the Prophets for the morning of the Day of Atonement is the passage of Isaiah from chap. lvii. 14 to the end of chap. lviii. The Babylonian Talmud (Megillah 31 a*) makes it begin at chap. lvii. 15. Parts of chap. lviii are given below from Professor Cheyne's *Isaiah* :—

'¹Call with the throat, hold not back; like a trumpet raise thy voice, and declare unto my people their rebellion, and unto the house of Jacob their sins. ²And (yet) me they consult daily, and to know my ways they desire: as a nation that hath done righteousness, and hath not forsaken the law of its God, they ask of me judgments of righteousness, the approach of God they desire. ³Wherefore have we fasted, and thou seest not—humbled our soul, and thou takest no notice? Behold, in your fasting ye pursue business, and all your tasks ye exact. ⁴Behold, it is for strife and contention ye fast, and to smite with the fist of wickedness: ye do not so fast at this time as to make your voice to be heard in the height. ⁵Can such be the fast that I choose, the day when a man humbleth his soul? Is it to bow down one's head like a bulrush, and to make sackcloth and ashes his couch? Wilt thou call this a fast, and a day acceptable to Jehovah? Is not this the fast that I choose—to loose the bands of wickedness, to untie the thongs of the yoke, and to set them that are crushed at liberty, and that ye burst in sunder every yoke? . . .
⁹If thou remove from the midst of thee the yoke, the stretching out of the finger, and speaking wickedness, and minister thy sustenance to the hungry, and satisfy the humbled soul.'

'¹³If thou turn thy foot from the Sabbath, so as not to do thy business on my holy day, and call the Sabbath a delight, the holy thing of Jehovah honourable, and honour it, so as not to do after thy wont, nor pursue thy

---

* ביום הכפורים קורין אחרי מות ומפטירין כי כה אמר רם ונשא ובמנחה קורץ בעריות ומפטירין ביונה.

business, nor speak words; [14] then shalt thou delight thyself in Jehovah ... for the mouth of Jehovah hath spoken it.'

This chapter on fasting and sabbatizing perfectly suits the day of the great Fast, which was also a great Sabbath. The description of true fasting as including (like sabbath-keeping) abstinence from worldly business as well as from sin, suggests the expression 'fast from the world'; and to keep the fast of fasts is, in the language of Leviticus, to 'sabbatize a sabbath.' Well-known words of the Law and the Prophets thus account for the substance and the form of the sayings (A) and (B) and for their inclusion in the same section of the Logia. The sabbath is of course on its positive side a feast and 'a delight,' although negatively of the nature of a fast.

The two component sayings of the Logion, each with its own parallelism, make up a symmetrical whole.

In (A) the renunciation of the world contrasts with finding the kingdom of God.

In (B) sabbatizing the sabbath forms a good parallel to seeing the Father, as in the Old Testament to keep one of the great festivals was to appear before God. Compare Deut. xvi. 16, and Isaiah i. 12 לראות פני with Professor Cheyne's translation and notes.

In (A) and (B) together (1) spiritual fasting and sabbatizing are up to a certain point identical, or cover the same ground; and (2) in contrast with τοῦ κόσμου the new sabbath is ἄλλου κόσμου ἀρχή, according to *Epist. Barn.* xv. 8 (trans. G. H. Rendall): 'Furthermore He saith unto them, "Your new moons and Sabbaths I cannot away with." Look ye how He saith, "Your present Sabbaths are not acceptable unto me, but *the Sabbath* which I have made (ἀλλὰ ὁ πεποίηκα), in the which, when I have finished all things, I will make the beginning of the eighth day, which is the beginning of a new world." Wherefore also we keep the eighth day unto gladness, in the which Jesus also rose from the dead, and after that He had been manifested, ascended into the heavens.' Note also (3) the parallelism between finding the Kingdom and seeing the King (τὸν πατέρα or τὸν Θεόν), comparing in Clem. *Quis Div. Salv.* § 19 (p. 14, ed. P. M. Barnard in *Texts and Studies*, 1897) ἵνα καθαρὸς τῇ καρδίᾳ γενόμενος ἴδῃς τὸν θεόν, ὅπερ καὶ δι' ἑτέρας φωνῆς ἐστὶν εἰσελθεῖν εἰς τὴν βασιλείαν τῶν οὐρανῶν.

Dr. Abbott (p. 11) writes, with reference to sayings of SS. Justin Martyr and Clement of Alexandria on ideal sabbatizing and fasting: 'These words imply a feast following a fast, a feast in God's kingdom following a fast in the age of this present world. Clearly Clement does not mean that the feast is to be deferred till after death. Feast and fast alike are to take place in this present life.'

Looking back as from the world to come, the Midrash contrasts it with the present, thus: 'This world is like a sabbath, and the world from which thou camest is like the sabbath eve: if a man provides not on the sabbath eve, what shall he eat on the sabbath? The world from which thou camest is like dry land, and this world like sea: if a man provides not for himself on the land, what shall he eat on the sea? This world is like a wilderness, and the world from which thou camest is like inhabited land; if a man provides not for himself from the inhabited land, what shall he eat in the wilderness?' See *Sayings of the Jewish Fathers*, chap. iv. note 28, on the saying, 'This world is like a vestibule before the world to come; prepare thyself at the vestibule, that thou mayest be admitted into the hall.'

Saith Jesus.

The several Logia after the first, which is defective at the beginning, are introduced by the formula ΛΕΓΕΙ ΙΗΣΟΥΣ, *Saith Jesus*.

The present tense 'Saith' marks the Logia as 'a collection of sayings having a present living force,' as Professor Lock has well observed. Another writer adds that ΛΕΓΕΙ is appropriate because the sayings purport to be 'living oracles of the living Lord,' like the inspired utterances cited from the Old Testament in the New, and introduced by a simple 'Saith,' or 'Saith the Scripture,' or 'the Spirit,' or 'the Lord.' Such may be the significance of 'Saith Jesus.' But 'Saith' may be used of any saying for which the authority is documentary. ' In ordinary Greek λέγει would naturally introduce a quotation from a book—ἔφη being the usual word when the quotation is a matter of history or tradition' (Bywater). Citations being innumerable and the uses of formulae of citation various, it must suffice here to illustrate some of the uses of λέγει by a few examples from the New Testament, the patristic writings, and Jewish tradition.

1. THE NEW TESTAMENT.

What is remarkable in the Logiographer's use of 'Saith Jesus' is that it is uniform and systematic, the same formula introducing every complete section of the Logia. This, as regards the λέγει, is illustrated by Rev. ii. 1—iii. 14:

'To the angel of the church in Ephesus write; These things *saith* he that holdeth the seven stars in his right hand, he that walketh in the midst of the seven golden candlesticks... And to the angel of the church in Smyrna write; These things *saith* the first and the last, which was dead, and lived again... And to the angel of the church in Pergamum write; These things *saith* he that hath the sharp two-edged sword... And to the angel of the church in Thyatira write; These things *saith* the Son of God, who hath his eyes like a flame of fire, and his feet are like unto burnished brass... And to the angel of the church in Sardis write; These things *saith* he that hath the seven Spirits of God... And to the angel of the church in Philadelphia write; These things *saith* he that is holy, he that is true, he that hath the key of David, he that openeth, and none shall shut, and that shutteth, and none openeth... And to the angel of the church in Laodicea write; These things *saith* the Amen, the faithful and true witness, the beginning of the creation of God.'

Here we have ΛΕΓΕΙ uniformly, and, as it happens, just as many times as there are Logia on the papyrus, if seven be their number, and not eight. If the epithets of the Lord in His Epistles to the Churches were summed up in the name Jesus, we should have ΛΕΓΕΙ ΙΗCΟΥC in every case, and in all seven times. The sayings thus introduced are meant to have a present living force, and they were dictated for the purpose of being written down. It is Jesus Himself who, by the hand of St. John, writes λέγει, as, in the Gospels, some of His sayings begin with a λέγω, *I say*.

2. THE PATRISTIC WRITINGS.

IRENAEUS.—Bishop J. B. Lightfoot, in discussing the genuineness of the Epistles of St. Ignatius, had occasion to investigate the usage of St. Irenaeus in introducing quotations; and he came to the conclusion that 'incomparably the most usual form of introducing quotations is some modification of *saying*, as λέγει, ἔλεγεν, φησίν, εἴρηκεν, εἶπεν, and in the Latin *dicit, dicebat, dixit, inquit, ait, refert*, with other parts of these same verbs.... The rationale of the tenses in introducing quotations is as follows; (i) The present *says* (λέγει, φησίν, &c.) can only be used where the reference is to *an extant writing*. It is most commonly employed of the literary author of the work, as Isaiah, David, Paul, Luke. But it is also used of any person who occupies a prominent place in the writing quoted and whose words are permanently recorded, as especially of Christ in the Gospels. The perfect (εἴρηκεν) is used in the same way as the present, and always implies a written document*. (ii) On the other hand the aorist *said* (εἶπεν, ἔφη) may be used equally of a written document and of oral tradition.'

It had been argued by Daillé that Irenaeus (v. 28) when, quoting from the letter of Ignatius to the Romans, he wrote, 'As one of our people said when condemned ... to wild beasts, *I am wheat of God, and I am ground by the teeth of wild beasts, that I may be found pure bread*,' must

---

* So the Hebrew שנאמר (abbrev. 'שנ), *for it hath been said*, introduces only quotations from the Bible.

have been referring to an unwritten saying, because he used 'said' instead of 'wrote' in introducing it.

AN ANCIENT HOMILY.—The so-called Second Epistle of St. Clement to the Corinthians is given in Bishop Lightfoot's *Apostolic Fathers* (ed. Harmer, 1891) as 'An Ancient Homily by an unknown author.' In the translation we read:—

'3. Yea, He Himself saith, *Whoso confesseth Me, him will I confess before the Father*. This then is our reward, if verily we shall confess Him through whom we were saved. But wherein do we confess Him? When we do that which He saith and are not disobedient unto His commandments, and not only *honour Him with our lips, but with our whole heart and with our whole mind*. Now He saith also in Isaiah, *This people honoureth Me with their lips, but their heart is far from Me*. 4. Let us therefore not only call Him Lord, for this will not save us, for He saith, *Not every one that saith unto Me, Lord, Lord, shall be saved, but he that doeth righteousness*. So then, brethren, let us confess Him in our works. 5. Wherefore, brethren, let us forsake our sojourn in this world and do the will of Him that called us, and let us not be afraid to depart out of this world. For the Lord saith, *Ye shall be as lambs in the midst of wolves*. 6. But the Lord saith, *No servant can serve two masters*. If we desire to serve both God and mammon, it is unprofitable for us: *For what advantage is it, if a man gain the whole world and forfeit his soul?* 8. For the Lord saith in the Gospel, *If ye kept not that which is little, who shall give unto you that which is great? For I say unto you that he which is faithful in the least, is faithful also in much*. 13. For the Lord saith, *Every way My Name is blasphemed among all the Gentiles*; and again, *Woe unto him by reason of whom My Name is blasphemed*. . . For when they hear from us that God saith, *It is no thank unto you, if ye love them that love you, but this is thank unto you, if ye love your enemies and them that hate you*; when they hear these things, I say, they marvel at their exceeding goodness.'

Logion II

§§ 3, 4, 6, 8. Compare in the Gospels, *These twelve Jesus sent forth, and* charged *them, saying,* ... *Every one therefore who shall confess me before men*... (Matt. x. 5, 32). *And he opened his mouth and* taught *them, saying,* ... *Not every one that saith unto me, Lord, Lord,* ...' (Matt. v. 2, vii. 21). *And he* said *also unto his disciples, There was a certain rich man.* ... *And I say unto you, Make to yourselves friends of the mammon of unrighteousness*... *He that is faithful in that which is least is faithful also in much*... *No servant can serve two masters*... *Ye cannot serve God and mammon* (Luke xvi. 1, 9, 10, 13). *Then Jesus* said *unto his disciples,* ... *For what shall a man be profited, if he shall gain the whole world, and forfeit his soul?* (Matt. xvi. 24, 26; Mark viii. 34, 36).

Thus the Homilist repeatedly uses λέγει, *saith*, where the Evangelists used past tenses, as *said* or *taught saying*; and the motive of the change is made plain by his words. He is not concerned as a teacher with the merely historical fact that the Lord said this or that on this or that occasion, but ἀεὶ ζῇ ταῦτα, he quotes the oracles of Jesus as living rules of conduct: the Lord *saith*, therefore let us *do*. It has been the way of the preacher in quoting the Gospels from that day to this to say with the Logiographer, 'Jesus saith.' There is a well-known narrative use of the present, *saith*, in contrast with which the homiletic use of it may be called *didactic*.

A good illustration of this use of 'saith' has been pointed out in the Book of Common Prayer, 'Hear what comfortable words our Saviour Christ *saith* unto all that truly turn to him.... Hear also what Saint Paul *saith* ... Hear also what Saint John *saith*.'

§ 5. Here we have 'a close parallel' to St. Luke x. 2-3: *And he* said *unto them,* .. *behold, I send you forth as lambs in the midst of wolves.* 'As however Peter is not mentioned in the context, and as the continuation of the quotation is not found in the canonical Gospels, the whole passage was probably taken from some apocryphal source, perhaps the Gospel of the Egyptians' (Lightfoot).

§ 13. '*God saith.* The passage quoted therefore is regarded as one of τὰ λόγια τοῦ Θεοῦ' (Lightfoot), cf. earlier in § 13, τὰ ἔθνη γάρ, ἀκούοντα ἐκ τοῦ στόματος ἡμῶν τὰ λόγια τοῦ Θεοῦ, ὡς καλὰ καὶ μεγάλα θαυμάζει. The 'Logion of God' here cited is given in substance as a saying of Jesus in St. Luke vi. 20, 27, 32, thus: *And he lifted up his eyes on his disciples, and said, ... But I say unto you, ... For if ye love them which love you, what thank have ye?*

HIPPOLYTUS.—Questions may be raised about the sources of several of the pseudo-Clement's citations, but it will be allowed that Hippolytus knew the Four Gospels. From this writer we will give one example of a λέγει substituted for an Evangelist's εἶπεν. In St. Matt. xxiv. 4, 12, 13 we read, *And Jesus answered and* said (εἶπεν) *unto them, ... And because iniquity shall abound, the love of many shall wax cold. But he that shall endure unto the end, the same shall be saved.* Compare in Lagarde's *Hippol. Rom.*, Fragment 59 (p. 168, 1858), καθὼς καὶ ὁ δεσπότης λέγει Διὰ τὸ πληθυνθῆναι τὴν ἀνομίαν ψυγήσεται ἡ ἀγάπη τῶν πολλῶν ... ὡς εἶπεν ὁ δεσπότης Ὁ δὲ ὑπομείνας εἰς τέλος οὗτος σωθήσεται. Thus the writer in quoting verse 13 resumes the Evangelist's narrative εἶπεν (Mark xiii. 5 ἤρξατο λέγειν), which he had changed into a didactic λέγει in quoting verse 12.

THE TWO CLEMENTS. St. Clement of Rome, imitating a formula of citation used by St. Paul, writes in chap. xiii of his Epistle to the Corinthians, 'most of all remembering the words of the Lord Jesus which He spake, teaching forbearance and long-suffering; for thus He SAID (εἶπεν); *Have mercy, that ye may receive mercy: forgive, that it may be forgiven to you. As ye do, so shall it be done to you ...*' St. Clement of Alexandria, changing εἶπεν into φησίν, writes, '*Have mercy,* SAITH *the Lord &c.*' (Strom. ii. 18). The Roman Clement's εἶπεν is consistent with the hypothesis of some critics that 'he derived the saying from oral tradition.'

Logion II

The Jewish Fathers.

Sayings of Jewish Rabbis were introduced by short formulae which have been compared with the Logiographer's 'Saith Jesus' (L. S. p. 47). Thus in Pirké Aboth, as translated by Mr. Singer, it is said, 'Hillel and Shammai received the tradition from the preceding. Hillel *said*, Be of the disciples of Aaron, loving peace and pursuing peace, loving thy fellow-creatures and drawing them near to the Torah. He *used to say* ... He *used to say* ... ,' where OMER, *said*, is an abbreviation of HAYAH OMER, *used to say*, lit. *was saying*. Such sayings were so quoted on the authority of oral tradition, the frequentative past expressing that a saying which it introduces was insisted upon as formulating a rule or principle of general application. Thus the Rabbinic 'used to say' and the Greek didactic 'saith,' of which examples have been given, agree except as to the authority for the sayings quoted, which the one makes oral and the other documentary.

At the beginning of Pirké Aboth, it is recorded that the men of the Great Synagogue *said* three things, or spake three words, a past tense (אמרו) being used of their utterances as of the Ten Words in Deut. v. 19 (דָּבָר).

Next we read in successive verses, 'Simon Justus was of the remnants of the Great Synagogue. *He used to say* ...' 'Antigonus of Socho received from Simon Justus. *He used to say* ...' 'Joseph ben Joezer of Zeredah and Joseph ben Jochanan of Jerusalem received from them. Joseph ben Joezer of Zeredah *said* (אומר) ... Joseph ben Jochanan of Jerusalem *said* ...' Thus the full formula of quotation comprises a short account of the Rabbi quoted, followed by '*He used to say.*' Later in the collection single sayings are quoted briefly in the form, ' Rabbi Lazar ben Azariah *said* (אומר) ... ,' and additional sayings, as of Hillel, in the form, '*He used to say.*'

Sayings of the Jewish Fathers, chap. iv, note 19, quotes from Talmud Babli *Berachoth* 17 a, ' It was *a commonplace in the mouth of* Raba that, The perfection of wisdom is repentance.' The synonym for '*He used to say*,' which introduces this saying of Raba in the Gemara, occurs also a few lines before and a few lines after it.

The narrative past, as in 'Diogenes *said* to Alexander,' is of course used also in Rabbinic in suitable contexts. For an example and a contrast see in chap. ii. of Pirké Aboth, ' Five disciples were there to Rabban Jochanan ben Zacchai... *He used to say* ... He *said* to them ...'

IV

LOGIA III-IV.

Λέγει 'Ιησοῦς,

(A) Ἔστην ἐν μέσῳ τοῦ κόσμου, καὶ ἐν σαρκὶ ὤφθην αὐτοῖς, καὶ εὗρον πάντας μεθύοντας καὶ οὐδένα εὗρον διψῶντα ἐν αὐτοῖς.

καί,

(B) Πονεῖ ἡ ψυχή μου ἐπὶ τοῖς υἱοῖς τῶν ἀνθρώπων, ὅτι τυφλοί εἰσιν τῇ καρδίᾳ αὐτῶν καὶ οὐ βλέπουσιν ... τὴν πτωχείαν.

Here we venture to depart from Messrs. Grenfell and Hunt's arrangement of the text (p. 5), which others also have called in question (L. S. p. 9), and to include the first editors' third and fourth Logia in a single section of like structure with Logion II, made up of a saying (A) introduced by 'Saith Jesus,' and a saying (B) which includes Logion IV, and is introduced by an editorial 'And.'

(A)

I stood in the midst of the world, and in flesh I was seen of them; and I found all drunken, and none found I athirst among them.

The retrospective character of the saying is remarkable. At what period, if any, of His life on earth could our Lord have spoken thus of having once been manifested in the flesh? Hebrews v. 7 looks back to 'the days of his flesh' from after the Ascension; and to that later time it is natural to assign the saying (A), comparing the words of Jesus spoken to St. Paul, and His words to St. John in the Apocalypse.

'First impressions are sometimes more trustworthy than those which are derived from study and argument. And in spite of what has been said in various quarters, I cannot think that the opening words ἔστην ἐν μέσῳ τοῦ κόσμου καὶ ἐν σαρκὶ ὤφθην αὐτοῖς could ever have come from our Lord. "To come" or "appear" or "be manifested in the flesh" is a phrase which belongs to the later Apostolic age—to the Pastoral Epistles and the Epistles of St. John (1 Tim. iii. 16; 1 John iv. 2; 2 John 7). It is a product of reflective theology looking back upon the Incarnation, and is unlike the language which our Lord Himself used while among men.' So Professor Sanday in L. S. p. 36.

The saying (A) was probably suggested by Baruch iii. 37, μετὰ τοῦτο ἐπὶ τῆς γῆς ὤφθη καὶ ἐν τοῖς ἀνθρώποις συνανεστράφη, R.V. *Afterward did she appear upon earth, and was conversant with men,* 'a passage which was applied by several of the early Fathers to Christ's sojourn upon earth' (G. H.). They so applied it after the Ascension, and the point of view in a Logion suggested by it would naturally be the same.

The verse of Baruch, in the opinion of Professor Swete, 'can hardly be without connexion with our *logion.*' But it 'belongs to the second part of that book, which is probably a later addition to the Hebrew Baruch; and this particular verse has been regarded by some recent scholars as a Christian interpolation.' Its use in the Logion (it is added) may suggest doubts as to the genuineness of the saying, the words of Baruch forming 'a tempting basis for an imaginary utterance of Christ.' 'Whether it is a genuine saying of our Lord, or the product of early meditation upon His true sayings and on the miracle of His life, we shall perhaps never know.'

μεθύοντας, *drunken*] Clem. *Quis Dives*, § 18 οὕτως καὶ

ἄπορός τις ὢν καὶ ἄβιος εὑρεθείη ποτ' ἂν μεθύων ταῖς ἐπιθυμίαις, καὶ χρήμασι πλούσιος νήφων καὶ πτωχεύων ἡδονῶν, πεπεισμένος, συνετός, καθαρός, κεκολασμένος, the poor may be *drunken* with desires, and the rich a pauper in pleasures.

διψῶντα, *athirst*] St. Matt. v. 6 διψῶντες τὴν δικαιοσύνην, cf. Rev. vii. 16, Ps. xlii. 2, lxiii. 1, Isa. xlix. 10, lv. 1. The saying (A) is illustrated by St. John vii. 37: 'Jesus stood and cried, saying, If any man *thirst*, let him come unto me, and drink;' and by the prediction that, as in the days of Noah and Lot men were 'eating and drinking,' so should it be at the Son of Man's second coming (Matt. xxiv. 37-39; Luke xvii. 26-28). The Logion makes Jesus say that so it was at His first coming: all were eating and drinking, and there was not one athirst.

(B)

My soul grieveth over the sons of men, because they are blind in their heart ... poverty.

There being little or nothing quite legible in the MS. between 'their heart' and 'poverty,' recourse must be had to conjecture to fill up the hiatus.

In *The Oxyrhynchus Papyri* it is said, 'Many critics have wished to connect τὴν πτωχείαν, our Logion IV, with the preceding saying. Of the various conjectures, we prefer Dr. Taylor's βλέ|[πουσιν αὐτῶν τὴν ταλαι|πωρίαν καὶ τ]ὴν πτωχείαν. But we must enter a protest against the current view that there is an *a priori* probability in favour of only one line being lost at the bottom of the *verso*. The lacuna may have extended to five or even ten lines.... Since there is nothing whatever to show the extent of the lacuna, any attempt to fill it up must be purely hypothetical. And a conjecture which presupposes a definite number of lines is thereby rendered very doubtful.'

In the text as read in G. H. (pp. 8-9) the *verso* ends :—

OTI TYΦΛOI EICIN TH KAP
ΔIA AYTω[N] KAI . . BΛEIC
. . . .

Logia III–IV

and the *recto* begins :—

[. . . .] . . [. T]HN ΠΤωΧΙΑ

the letters dotted below being doubtful.

With a transposition of the words αὐτῶν τὴν ταλαιπωρίαν, I propose now to read after καρδίᾳ αὐτῶν,

καὶ οὐ βλέπουσιν τὴν ταλαιπωρίαν αὐτῶν καὶ τὴν πτωχείαν,

but with the termination αν abbreviated in both cases, thus,

KAI OY BΛE
ΠΟΥCΙΝ ΤΗΝ ΤΑΛΑΙΠωΡΙΑ
ΑΥΤωΝ ΚΑΙ ΤΗΝ ΠΤωΧΙΑ

The scribe's mistake of writing at first ΙΑ without Є in the last word is accounted for by the hypothesis that there was ΙΑ just above.

The words βλέπουσιν and ταλαιπωρίαν were arrived at successively as follows :—

1. A view of the papyrus suggested that the doubtful βλεις might be read as above, and after 'blind' would come quite naturally 'and see not,' as in Acts xiii. 11 we read τυφλὸς μὴ βλέπων, 'and thou shalt be *blind, not seeing* the sun for a season.' Given that before βλε came καί followed by space for two letters (G. H.), the obvious, if not the only possible, reading was καὶ οὐ βλέπουσιν.

2. What is it that men 'see not'? Probably their 'poverty' (Log. IV) in the spiritual sense; for this would give the required parallelism between (A) and (B), the one saying expressing men's want of perception of their spiritual need in terms of satiety, the other calling this need 'poverty.' This, so far as it went, was confirmed, and something more was suggested by the following passages from the Apocalypse, a book which also supplies illustrations of 'thirst' in the spiritual sense (L. S. p. 10).

Rev. ii. 8–9: 'These things saith the first and the last, which was dead, and lived again: I know thy tribulation, and thy *poverty* (but thou art rich).'

Rev. iii. 14, 17–18: 'These things saith the Amen, the faithful and true witness, the beginning of the creation of

God. . . . Because thou sayest, I am rich, and have gotten riches, and have need of nothing; and knowest not that thou art the *wretched* one and miserable and *poor* and *blind* and naked: I counsel thee to buy of me gold refined by fire, that thou mayest become rich . . . and eyesalve to anoint thine eyes, that thou mayest *see.*'

Thus in Logia of Jesus to be written for the Churches of Asia, He uses the word 'poverty,' which is not in the Gospels; and He says in effect of the lukewarm Laodiceans that spiritually they were blind, and saw not their wretchedness and their poverty.

These considerations suggested that the saying (B) should perhaps be read somewhat as follows:—

My soul grieveth over the sons of men, because they are blind in their heart, and see not their wretchedness and their poverty.

In the apocryphal Gospel of Thomas (A. viii.) Jesus says:—

Let the blind in heart see.

(A) *and* (B).

Laying no stress upon arguments from the supposed original dimensions of the papyrus, such as, 'If the *recto* side had come first, there would have been good reason for thinking that the saying appeared in a shortened form, since it is unlikely that more than a few lines are lost at the bottom of the leaf' (G. H. p. 10, on Log. 1),—we include (A) and (B) in one section because they seem to be parallel and to fit together.

1.

Drunken, athirst, blind, poverty.] These expressions, taken in pairs in various ways, have a certain parallelism, which has already been partly illustrated. One saying (B) has been assumed to include two of them, 'blind' and 'poverty,' according to the analogy of a verse cited from the Apocalypse. Men are described as blind to their spiritual need, which the Logiographer (we suppose) goes

Logion V

on to describe in terms of poverty. We shall find 'blind' and 'poor' again in close connexion in a passage which will be cited from an Apocryphal Gospel.

2.

The Beatitudes in the Sermon on the Mount bring together them that 'hunger and thirst,' and 'the poor'; and Clem. *Quis Dives*, § 17 (Barnard, p. 13) writes in this connexion of them that 'thirst for the righteousness of God,' and adds that 'the opposite kind of poor are miserable, having no portion in God, still less in human possession, and being without taste of the righteousness of God.'

3.

In the next section of *Quis Dives*, quoted on pp. 27-28, notice again the contrast of μεθύων, *drunken*, and πτωχεύων.

4.

Drunken, blind. A parallel 'may be found in one of the Sibylline poems, describing the Jews during the crucifixion as *drunken* and as *blinder than moles*' (Abbott, p. 14). *Sib. Orac.*, i. 360-370, καὶ τότε δ' Ἰσραὴλ μεμεθυσμένος οὐχὶ νοήσει ... ἀτὰρ ὄμμασιν οὐκ ἐσορῶντες | τυφλότεροι σπαλάκων.

V

LOGION V.

Λέγει Ἰησοῦς,
(A) Ὅπου ἐὰν ὦσιν β' οὐκ εἰσὶν ἄθεοι καὶ ὅπου εἷς ἐστιν μόνος λέγω Ἐγώ εἰμι μετ' αὐτοῦ.

(B) Ἔγειρον τὸν λίθον κἀκεῖ εὑρήσεις με σχίσον τὸ ξύλον κἀγὼ ἐκεῖ εἰμί.

(A)

This saying is very defective in the MS., and has given rise to numerous conjectures. It is read as above by Professor Blass, whose restoration of it gives the sense:—

Wheresoever there be two, they are not godless; and where there is one only, I say, I am with him.

In the first edition of the Logia it was written thus:—

[ΛΕΓ]ΕΙ [ΙC ΟΠ]ΟΥ ΕΑΝ ѠCΙΝ
[....]Ε[...].. ΘΕΟΙ ΚΑΙ
[..]ϹΟ . Ε[..] ΕϹΤΙΝ ΜΟΝΟϹ
[..]ΤѠ ΕΓѠ ΕΙΜΙ ΜΕΤ ΑΥ
Τ[ΟΥ]

In the notes on the transcript in G. H. p. 13, it was said in effect that the letter before ΘΕΟΙ was Α, and of the doubtful C in the next line it was said that it might 'equally well' be the second half of Π. This line was accordingly read by Blass and others independently:—

ΟΠΟΥ ΕΙϹ ΕϹΤΙΝ ΜΟΝΟϹ
Where there is one only.

In contrast with 'where there is *one only* I am with him,' the preceding clause must have promised a Divine Presence to *more than one*; but it was very difficult to express this in words likely to have been used in the Logion, and which could be fitted into the small space at the decipherer's disposal. Messrs. Grenfell and Hunt supplied the data for a satisfactory reading in their note, 'It seems fairly certain that the Logion offers a general parallel to St. Matt. xviii. 20—"For where two or three are gathered together," &c.—though with considerable divergences. An extension of that verse which comes nearer to our passage is found in Ephraem Syr. *Evang. Concord. Expos.* c. 14 (*v.* Resch, *Agrapha*, p. 295), where the important addition *ubi unus est* corresponds to μόνος here, and suggests that ΕΙϹ should be read either at the beginning of l. 25 or before ΕϹΤΙΝ.'

The words of Ephraem as given by Resch in the Latin of Mösinger are:—

'Sicut in omnibus indigentiis gregi suo Christus consuluit, ita et vitam solitariam agentes in hac tristi conditione consolatus est dicens : *Ubi unus est, ibi et ego sum*, ne quisquam ex solitariis contristaretur, quia ipse est gaudium nostrum et ipse nobiscum est. *Et ubi duo sunt, ibi et ego ero*, quia misericordia et gratia eius nobis obumbrat. Et quando tres sumus, quasi in ecclesiam coimus, quae est corpus Christi perfectum et imago eius expressa.'

The 'two' are twice mentioned in St. Matt. xviii. 19–20: 'Again I say unto you, that if two of you shall agree on earth as touching anything that they shall ask, it shall be done for them of my Father which is in heaven. For where two or three are gathered together in my name, there am I in the midst of them.'

Ephraem, in order to lead up to 'three,' which make an *ecclesia*, mentions the one before the two, thus:—

Ubi unus est, ibi et ego sum,
Et ubi duo sunt, ibi et ego ero.

If there had been no mention of the three, it would have been more natural to place the two before the one, thus:—

Ubi duo sunt . . . Et ubi unus est . . . ;

that is to say, where there are two, and even where there is only one, Christ is present. This suggests a way of completing the first part of (A), which the first editors practically read,

ΟΠΟΥ ΕΑΝ ѠCIN . . . . Ε . . . . ΑΘΕΟΙ

each dot standing for one missing letter.

Reading εἰσὶν ἄθεοι, *they are godless,* and then prefixing the negative οὐκ, we have space before it for a single letter, which Blass ingeniously fills with the numeral β´, *two* (L. S. p. 22), thus giving the sense,

Wheresoever there be two, they are not godless,

and making (A) as a whole agree in substance with the traditional saying of Christ preserved by Ephraem. Mr. Redpath shews (L. S. p. 39), that 'even in a calligraphic MS. like Cod. Vaticanus it is possible to have a numeral represented by a letter and another spelt out in full side by side.'

λέγω] On the [..]ΤѠ in the first transcript it is said in G. H. p. 13, 'In l. 26 the first letter of which any part is preserved may be Τ, Π, or Γ; but [Ε]ΓѠ would not fill the lacuna.' It is of no very obvious importance for the general sense how we fill it; but it may be remarked in favour of λέγω that it introduces sayings of Jesus in the Gospels, as for example in St. Matthew, loc. cit., 'Again I say unto you, that if two &c.'

ἄθεοι] Eph. ii. 11 : 'Wherefore remember, that aforetime ye, the Gentiles in the flesh, who are called Uncircumcision by that which is called Circumcision, in the flesh, made by hands; that ye were at that time *separate from Christ*, alienated from the commonwealth of Israel, and strangers from the covenants of the promise, having no hope and ἄθεοι ἐν τῷ κόσμῳ, *without God in the world*.' As here 'separate from Christ' and 'without God' stand in parallelism, so in (A) we have in parallel clauses οὐκ εἰσὶν ἄθεοι and 'Ἐγώ εἰμι μετ' αὐτοῦ, the two are *not without-God* and Jesus is with the one. From this Harnack infers (p. 21), 'dass in dem Evangelium, aus welchem unser Spruch stammt, Gott und Christus sich besonders nahe gerückt waren.' This may be a correct inference. But we shall have also to consider a different interpretation of the curious double negative in οὐκ ἄθεοι, *not without* God.

Pirké Aboth.

Some well-known sayings in the third chapter of Aboth are thus translated in *Sayings of the Jewish Fathers*:—

'R. Chalafta of Kaphar-Chananiah said, When *ten* sit and are occupied in words of Torah the Shechinah is among them, for it is said, God standeth in the congregation of the mighty (Ps. lxxxii. 1). And whence (is it proved of) even *five*? Because it is said, He judgeth among gods. And whence even *three*? Because it is said, . . . and hath founded his troop in the earth (Amos ix. 6). And whence even *two*? Because it is said, Then they that feared the Lord spake often the one to the other (Mal. iii. 16). And whence even *one*? Because it is said, In all places where I record my name I will come unto thee, and I will bless thee (Exod. xx. 24).'

The first of these sayings simply means that the Shechinah is with a congregation, the number *ten* being

Logion V

the conventional quorum in accordance with Num. xiv. 27, 'How long shall I bear with this evil congregation?' From the twelve spies take away Joshua and Caleb, and there remain ten. Ten persons therefore make a congregation. Rabbi Isaac in *Talm. Babli Berachoth*, 6 *a*, says, 'The Holy One is found in the synagogue, for it is said, God standeth in the congregation of El.' In *Sanhedrin*, 39 *a*, an unbeliever asks, 'If every assembly of ten has its Shechinah, how many Shechinahs are there?'

The saying about the *five* is doubtless a comparatively late addition.

The saying about the *two* is also given earlier in the same chapter, thus: 'R. Chananiah ben Tradyon said, Two that sit together without words of Torah are a session of scorners, for it is said, Nor sitteth in the seat of the scornful (Ps. i. 1); but two that sit together and are occupied in words of Torah have the Shechinah among them, for it is said, Then they that feared the Lord &c.' Possibly the saying in St. Matt. xviii. 19, '... if two of you shall agree ... as touching anything that they shall ask, it shall be done for them,' alludes to the same verse of Scripture as this rabbinic saying, i.e. Mal. iii. 16, 'Then they that feared the Lord spake often *the one to the other: and the Lord hearkened and heard.*'

The rabbinic proof for the case of the *one* is from an idiom frequent in the Old Testament, the collective or distributive use of the singular instead of the plural, the particular passage referred to being Exod. xx. 22–25: 'And the Lord said unto Moses, Thus thou shalt say unto the children of Israel, Ye yourselves have seen that I have talked with you from heaven. Ye shall not make with me gods of silver, neither shall ye make unto you gods of gold. An altar of earth thou shalt make unto me, and shalt sacrifice thereon ... *in every place where I record my name I will come unto thee*, and I will bless thee. And if thou wilt make me an altar of stone, thou shalt not build it of hewn stone: for if thou lift up thy tool upon it, thou hast polluted it.'

What is written is for Israel generally, but it applies to 'even one,' because it is said, 'I will come unto THEE.' Other passages might have been cited for this use of the singular, but there was none better for the purpose than this, in which it is written that *in every place* where mention is made of His Name the Lord will be present even with the one. There is a rabbinic saying that *the Shechinah is in every place*. The saying, 'And whence even one &c.' being merely a saying of Scripture rabbinicized, may have been current in some form as one of the sayings of the Fathers at a very early date. As a verse of Pirké Aboth it is still read on Sabbath afternoons in the Synagogues of the Ashkenazic Jews.

The *Midrash* on Deuteronomy (Deut. Rab. ii. 16) tells a story of a ship manned by heathens, except one Jew. Touching at an island, they commission him to buy things for them. He objects that he is a stranger and does not know his way about. They reply, 'Can a Jew be a stranger anywhere, when whithersoever thou goest thy God is with thee, For what nation is there so great, who hath God so nigh *unto him*?' the singular אליו (Deut. iv. 7) used of the nation being applied to a solitary member of it. In Neo-Hebrew גוי, ἔθνος, may mean *a heathen*.

THE DIDACHÉ.

Chapter iv of the Didaché begins thus: ' My child, him that speaketh to thee the word of God thou shalt remember night and day, ... *for whence the Lordship is spoken, there the Lord is*, ὅθεν γὰρ ἡ κυριότης λαλεῖται ἐκεῖ κύριός ἐστιν.'

On this it was remarked in the writer's *Two Lectures* on the Teaching of the Twelve Apostles, ' In the *Apostolical Constitutions* this takes the simpler and less idiomatic form, *for where the teaching concerning God is, there God is present.* Following the clue given by this paraphrase we are led, as it will be shewn, by way of a series of rabbinical sayings to a text from the Pentateuch on which the saying now under discussion may have been founded ... The above-mentioned paraphrase ... exactly agrees with

Logion V

a favourite principle of the Jewish Fathers, that those who sit and occupy themselves with words of "Torah," that is, the Law of the Lord, have the Shechinah amongst them. At the end of a series of sayings to that effect, in connexion with the numbers of *ten, five, three* and *two* persons so assembled, it is asked in the third chapter of the tract Aboth, What is the evidence that the Divine Presence will be vouchsafed even to *one*, who sits alone and meditates on the Law? and a proof is given from Exodus xx. 24, *In all places where I shall cause mention to be made of my name, I will come unto thee, and I will bless thee.* Where the name of the Lord is uttered, ... there the Lord is.'

The New Testament.

St. John xiv. 22-23: 'Judas saith unto him, not Iscariot, Lord, how is it that thou wilt manifest thyself unto us, and not unto the world? Jesus answered and said unto him, If a man (ἐάν τις) love me, he will keep my words : and my Father will love him, and *we will come unto him*, and make our abode with him.'

Rev. iii. 20 (cf. Cant. v. 2): 'Behold, I stand at the door, and knock : if any man (ἐάν τις) hear my voice, and open the door, *I will come in to him*, and will sup with him, and he with me.'

These sayings seem to rest upon Exodus, loc. cit., the remarkable words of Jesus, 'we will come,' 'I will come,' corresponding to the words of the Lord in that passage of the Old Testament, 'I will come unto thee, and I will bless thee.' The same verse may possibly be referred to in the saying, 'For where two or three are gathered together *in my name*, there am I in the midst of them.'

The saying, *And where there is one alone I am with him* is of course in substance a genuine Logion of Jesus, but we may doubt whether its words are His words. When He said, 'and lo, I am with you alway, even unto the end of the world' (Matt. xxviii. 20), the assurance of His presence was for 'one alone' as well as for two or more together, fulfilling His command to make disciples of the nations.

But He also says explicitly, according to the Fourth Gospel and the Apocalypse as cited above, that He will be with any one (τις) who loves Him, or hears His voice. Thus the Oxyrhynchus saying, 'And where there is one alone I am with him,' even if it were a genuine saying of Jesus, would not be a substantial addition to the sayings of the Lord preserved in the New Testament Scriptures.

(B)

Raise up the stone, and there thou shalt find me; cleave the tree, and there am I.

ἔγειρον] 'Though unable to offer any better suggestion, we are somewhat less confident than we were about the correctness of the reading ἔγειρον. The ο seems to be joined by a ligature to the preceding letter, which we should therefore expect to be σ rather than ρ. But the apparent ligature might be accounted for by supposing that the ο was badly written' (*Oxyrhynchus Papyri*). To read EΞAPON is anything but 'sehr möglich,' the *gamma* in the first editors' reading being apparently not doubtful, and *xi* not in the least resembling that letter.

The word ἐγείρειν means in various senses to *raise up*, as from sleep or death. It is used 'of buildings, *to raise, construct, erect:* τὸν ναόν, Jn. ii. 19 sq. ... 1 Esdr. v. 43; Sir. xlix. 13; Lat. *excito turrem ... sepulchrum*' (Thayer, *N. T. Lex.*), cf. in 1 Esdr. v. 62 ἐπὶ τῇ ἐγέρσει, 'for the *raising up* of the house of the Lord.' The nearest Biblical parallel to ἐγείρειν λίθον is in the preaching of St. John the Baptist, 'for I say unto you, that God is able ἐκ τῶν λίθων τούτων ἐγεῖραι, *of these stones to raise up* children unto Abraham' (Matt. iii. 9; Luke iii. 8). Origen on St. John's Gospel (tom. vi. 27, p. 143, ed. Brooke), as Dr. E. A. Abbott on the Logia has pointed out, writes of the multitudes and the Pharisees, with reference to the Baptist's saying, πλὴν ἑκάτεροι τοὺς προειρημένους λίθους δεικνυμένους ἀκούουσιν δύνασθαι ἐγερθῆναι τέκνα τῷ Ἀβραάμ, ἀπὸ τῆς ἀναισθησίας καὶ νεκρότητος ἀναστησομένους.

Logion V

1.

The view of (B) 'which has been most widely accepted is that which sees in the words an assertion of Christ's presence in nature; so that the sequence of thought will be, " In all forms of human life I am present; yea, and under inanimate creation you will find Me." In this case the singular will be deictic; " Lift yonder stone, cleave yonder piece of wood." This is an assertion of Christ's universal presence, differing only in its vividness from the language of the prologue of St. John, or of Eph. i. 23, or of Ps. cxxxviii. 7, 8 : it does not deny Christ's personality or merge him in nature, though it must be admitted that it finds its closest analogies in the Gnostic writers whom we have quoted, and whose teaching tended to that issue' (L. S. p. 25).

In illustration of this, which has been called the *pantheistic* interpretation, we may compare near the end of Lucian's *Hermotimus* the teaching received by a young man from a philosopher and repeated at home, that God pervades all things, such as *trees* and *stones* and animals, even to the meanest, ἀκούομεν δὲ αὐτοῦ λέγοντος ὡς καὶ ὁ θεὸς οὐκ ἐν οὐρανῷ ἐστιν, ἀλλὰ διὰ πάντων πεφοίτηκεν, οἷον ξύλων καὶ λίθων καὶ ζῴων, ἄχρι καὶ τῶν ἀτιμοτάτων. If such teaching was in vogue when the Logia were current and when they were composed, it would not be surprising to find some trace of it in one of them. Does the saying *Raise up the stone &c.*, embody or allude to such teaching or any modification of it?

Such pantheism as that of the passage quoted from the *Hermotimus*, § 81, was characteristic of Stoicism; and from a close parallel in his writings recently quoted in the *Classical Review* (Nov. 1898) we may infer that Clem. Alex. regarded it as Stoic, and not the teaching of a Logion of Jesus. Mr. A. C. Pearson writes (cf. p. 53 n.) : 'The whole context in the *Hermotimus* is redolent of Stoicism, and the matter is put beyond dispute by a comparison with Clem. Alex. *Protrept.* 5, § 66 οὐδὲ μὴν τοὺς ἀπὸ τῆς Στοᾶς παρελεύσομαι διὰ πάσης ὕλης καὶ διὰ τῆς ἀτιμοτάτης τὸ θεῖον διήκειν λέγοντας, and Themist. de Anim. 72 b τάχα δὲ καὶ τοῖς ἀπὸ Ζήνωνος σύμφωνος ἡ δόξα διὰ πάσης οὐσίας πεφοιτηκέναι τὸν θεὸν τιθεμένοις.' The pantheistic view of the saying rests chiefly upon the word THERE, which (L. S. p. 24) 'points more naturally to the place than to the action, "Thou shalt find Me in the stone" rather than "in the act of raising."' But it has to be explained how by merely moving a stone one is to discover anything inside it. 'Raise the stone and thou shalt find'—presumably something that was underneath it. 'Cleave the tree'—and find something inside it. Whatever else may be found by raising a stone or splitting a tree, or by any sort of mechanical operation on inorganic matter, the presence of God or the Logos in the material things operated upon will not thereby be made perceptible in any sense in which it was not so before. If Jesus is to be found in stone and tree alike, why is the one to be raised and the other split? If His spirit pervades the tree, why cleave it? The difference of kind in the actions 'raise,' 'cleave' is hard to account for on the pantheistic hypothesis.

The argument from the word 'there' is not without force. On the other hand, it is to be observed that in the first part of the Logion Jesus is made to say in effect, 'Where two are, where one is, *there* am I,' in the sense of St. Matt. xviii. 20, 'For where two or three are gathered together in my name, *there* am I in the midst of them.' If the Logion is to be regarded as homogeneous and continuous, ἐκεῖ must have the same sense in (B) as in the verse cited from St. Matthew.

Origen on the words of the Baptist (John i. 26), 'In the midst of you standeth one whom ye know not,' expounds them of Christ invisibly present in His Divinity with every man, and extended over all the world: the same who as incarnate *was seen upon the earth and conversant with men* (Baruch): who as the Logos pervades (πεφοίτηκε διά) the whole creation, and is in the midst of

Logion V

men without being perceived or seen. He quotes Jer. xxiii. 24, 'Do not I fill heaven and earth? saith the Lord'; and he writes as he might have written if he knew Logion V and took the pantheistic view of (B).

Having said that Christ pervades the whole creation, he has said implicitly that He pervades trees and stones, as the philosopher's disciple says of 'the god' in the *Hermotimus*. Nevertheless, when in the same context Origen speaks expressly of stones, in words quoted above on p. 38, he takes them as very types of ἀναισθησία and deadness, in accordance with the uniform tenour of Scriptural teaching. 'Woe unto him that saith to the wood, Awake; to the dumb stone, Arise' (Hab. ii. 19).

2.

We may vary the pantheistic interpretation by supposing the stone and the tree to have a certain '*consécration*.'

(1) *Raise up the stone*] In Gen. xxviii. 11 sq. we read that Jacob 'took of the stones of the place, and put *them* (A.V.) under his head, and lay down in that place to sleep.' He has his dream of the ladder; the Lord says, *Behold, I am with thee*; and in the morning Jacob *set up the stone* for a pillar, and says, 'If God will be with me ... this stone, which I have set up for a pillar, shall be God's house.' If we could find an equally apt illustration of the remainder of (B), we might think that we had solved the mystery of the Logion. That Jacob's dream should be referred to in a Logion ascribed to our Lord is not unnatural, when it is referred to in His saying in St. John i. 51.

The Greek for *bethel*-stone is βαίτυλος or βαιτύλιον. On sacred stones see Professor Cheyne's note on Isa. lvii. 6: 'Among the smooth stones of the valley is thy portion; they, they are thy lot: even to them hast thou poured a drink offering, thou hast offered a meal offering.'

(2) *The tree*] In the *Midrash* on Exod. iii. 2, 'And the angel of the Lord appeared unto him in a flame of fire out of the midst of the bush,' it is said in *Ex. Rab.* ii. 5 that a heathen asked, Why did the Lord speak with Moses from

the thorn-bush? He is told that it was to show 'that there is no place vacant without Shechinah, not even a thorn-bush,' the meanest of 'trees.'

Expressed in the language of the first part of the Logion this amounts to saying that there is *not* a place that is *without-God*, with the kind of emphasis which the double negative seems to require. This, so far as it goes, illustrates the last clause of the Logion. But the question has still to be answered, Raising up the stone may make it a *bethel*, but what has hacking the tree to do with the manifestation of Jesus?

3.

Jesus having said that He will be present with 'two' of His disciples, and even with 'one alone,' His concluding words signify that He will be with them when they are engaged in raising 'the stone' or cleaving 'the wood,' whatever that may mean. It may be understood literally, or in some metaphorical sense.

(1) To Professor Swete a clue to the meaning seems to be suggested by Eccles. x. 9, ' Whoso removeth stones shall be hurt therewith ; and he that cleaveth wood shall be endangered thereby,' LXX ἐξαίρων λίθους διαπονηθήσεται ἐν αὐτοῖς· σχίζων ξύλα κινδυνεύσει ἐν αὐτοῖς.

'The writer is dealing with the toils and dangers inherent in the arts of life, which are minimised by the gift of wisdom. In building, the raising of the great blocks of which the temple or palace is constructed is a work of much labour; the cleaving of the timber, a work of peril. The Lord, if this *logion* be really His, adapts the saying of Koheleth to the circumstances connected with the spiritual building of His Church. His Apostles, scattered over the world, alone amongst unbelievers, would incur much hard labour and many perils. But it was just in such toilsome and dangerous work that they might expect the promised Presence of Christ. "Raise the stone, do the uphill work of the religious pioneer, and thou shalt find Me. Cleave the timber, face the danger that lies in the way of duty, and there am I." The Wisdom of God

(Eccl. x. 10) pledges Himself to be with the Christian builder, and never more so than when he builds alone, and with labour and peril. There is a true Christian *Gnosis* here, but no Gnosticism.'

(2) Dr. Abbott writes, on the stone and the tree, that 'the first step is to ascertain what Clement (our trusty guide so far) has to say about "stones and trees" from the Christian point of view.' According to him they are οἱ ἄφρονες, *the senseless (Cohort. ad Gentes,* Potter, p. 4); 'and he explains the saying that "God can raise up from these stones children to Abraham" as referring to men *petrified* in relation to truth. God, he says, has actually thus made men out of stones; they have, as it were, risen from the dead. Clement does not actually use the word "stones" as the grammatical object of "raise." But Origen does, when he speaks of the stones themselves as "able to be *raised up* (ἐγερθῆναι) [*as*] *children* to Abraham." Ignatius, and in much fuller detail Hermas, speak of the raising up of stones so as to build the tower of the Lord.' 'The elaborate metaphor points to an original basis of tradition (p. 20 n.) about "raising the stone."'

Compare in *The Witness of Hermas to the Four Gospels* (p. 114 sq.), 'As the Cross lifts up Christ, or the *temple* of His body (John ii. 21), so Ignatius makes it lift up the several stones of the spiritual temple; writing in *Ephes.* 9, as rendered by Bp. Lightfoot, "But I have learned that certain persons passed through you from yonder, bringing evil doctrine; whom ye suffered not to sow seed in you, for ye stopped your ears, so that ye might not receive the seed sown by them; forasmuch as ye are stones of a temple, which were prepared beforehand for a building of God the Father, being hoisted up to the heights through the engine of Jesus Christ, which is the Cross, and using for a rope the Holy Spirit; while your faith is your windlass, and love is the way that leadeth up to God." Very like this is the building of the tower upon the rock higher than the mountains in *Sim.* ix of Hermas.... In Lagarde's *Hippol. Rom.,* i. 59 (p. 30) the Church is likened to a ship. . . . It has *angels* for sailors, and the symbol of the Passion as *a ladder that leadeth up to the height, drawing* the faithful to the ascent of the heavens.' *Vis.* iii. 2. 6 (cf. 5. 2) speaks of stones *drawn* up from the deep and set in the building (ib. p. 117). 'The building of the tower is a sustained illustration of the words, *God is able of these stones &c.*' (ib. p. 33).

Dr. Abbott (p. 20) refers also to the Song of the Vineyard in Isaiah v. The Master is spoken of as digging it, clearing it of stones, and building a tower in it: 'and the stones would presumably be employed in building the "tower" and the walls round the vineyard. There is no mention of uprooting weeds or bushes, or of cutting down useless trees; but such work would often be a necessary part of the labour of preparing fresh land for culture.'

He quotes also Eccl. x. 8-10: 'He that diggeth a pit shall fall into it; and whoso breaketh through a fence, a serpent shall bite him. Whoso *heweth out* (or *removeth*) *stones* shall be hurt therewith; and he that *cleaveth trees* (or *wood*) is endangered thereby. If the iron be blunt, and one do not whet the edge, then must he put to more strength; but wisdom is profitable to direct,' as a passage to which the Logion may refer, and concludes as follows (p. 22):—

'Now, coming to the gospels, we have to ask whether in them "cleaving trees" and "raising up stones" are connected together in any sense that may harmonize with all the above-mentioned traditions, and also throw light on our Logion. The teaching of the Baptist will occur to many as supplying a parallel. The Jews are addressed by him as trees destined to be cut down unless they bring forth fruit; and the same passage speaks of "children of Abraham" as able to be raised up "from stones." Perhaps John was actually standing amid the objects of which he speaks—large stones embedded in the earth, useless bushes and trees cumbering the ground, the former demanding to be "lifted" into walls and buildings where they might help instead of hindering the agriculturist, the latter demanding to be cut down, hewn to pieces, and burned, since they were unfit for any other purpose. In any case, we can well understand that such doctrine, deeply impressed on the Baptist's disciples and taken up by Jesus, may have found expression in such a saying as our papyrus has preserved. If so, the meaning of it is, in effect: "Raise up the fallen soul and place it as a living stone in the tower of the vineyard. Cut down and cleave the barren bushes and trees of hypocrisy, malignity, avarice, and selfishness. Wherever thou art doing this, either in thine own heart, or among the sons of men, there am I present with thee."'

τὸ ξύλον] Dr. Abbott (p. 15) investigates the uses of ξύλον in singular and plural, with or without the article, in Biblical Greek, and concludes that τὸ ξύλον in the Logion should mean not 'the wood' but 'the tree.' 'There is probably no instance in the LXX, and certainly none in the New Testament, where τὸ ξύλον used absolutely means *wood*,'—like ξύλον and ξύλα without the article; or τὸ ξύλον when defined by the context as the wood of something, as an axe or a specified 'tree' or kind of tree, cf. Lev. xiv. 6 LXX τὸ ξύλον τὸ κέδρινον, Heb. *of the cedar*.

Notice the ambiguity in Deut. xix. 4-5: 'And this is the case of the manslayer . . . as when a man goeth into the forest . . . to hew wood (LXX συναγαγεῖν ξύλα), and his hand fetcheth a stroke with the axe to cut down the tree (τὸ ξύλον), and the iron slippeth from the wood (καὶ ἐκπεσὸν τὸ σιδήριον ἀπὸ τοῦ ξύλου, i.e. *the wood* of the axe, or *the tree*), and lighteth upon his neighbour, that he die; he shall flee unto one of these cities and live.'

At the end of his note Dr. Abbott writes, 'These considerations suggest at the outset that τὸ ξύλον here (in Logion V) means the stock or stump of some useless tree, possibly with a play on the meaning of lifelessness and helplessness conveyed by its association with "stone".'

(3) Professor Harnack, connecting the saying (B) with Eccles. x. 9 (p. 42, § 3), interprets it quite literally, 'Do the simplest work, quarry stone or cut down trees, and you will find My presence with you' (L. S. p. 24). As against

the 'illustration' from Ecclesiastes, it is asked in L. S., 'Why ἐγείρειν for ἐξαίρειν? ... why τὸν λίθον, τὸ ξύλον for λίθους and ξύλα? why the aorist tenses?,' ἔγειρον, σχίσον. 'Such an allusion would almost necessitate ἔξαιρε λίθους, σχίζε ξύλα ... the aorists point to one action rather than to a regular occupation.'

This is not merely an objection to the illustration from Ecclesiastes, which may or may not be appropriate, but an argument for making the Logion refer to some one stone and some one tree.

But it may be said, the singulars *stone, tree,* preceded by the aorist tenses are 'deictic.' 'Lift yonder stone, cleave yonder piece of wood' (L. S. p. 25), or tree. In a graphic style of writing or in a picture, one block of stone or one tree may serve typically for stones or trees, one only being supposed to come into the field of view at once. A woodcutter felling trees is at any instant engaged upon a single tree, as in the case supposed in Deut. xix. 5, where a man goes into a wood to hew עצים, trees, 'and his hand fetcheth a stroke with the axe to cut down *the tree.*'

Compare 2 Kings vi. 1-5: 'And the sons of the prophets said unto Elisha ... Let us go, we pray thee, unto Jordan, and take thence every man one beam ... And when they came to Jordan they cut τὰ ξύλα. And the one was felling *the beam* (τὴν δοκόν), and the iron fell into the water: and he cried, and said, Alas, my master! for it was borrowed.' The one was felling *the beam* that he was to fell; or according to the English Bible, ' one was felling *a beam.'*

In accordance with Biblical usage, it would seem that the saying (B) might mean and be paraphrased, 'Raise stones, cleave trees.' A singular in Hebrew has often to be translated by a plural in English, as in Gen. iii. 8, 'And the man and his wife hid themselves from the presence of the Lord God amongst *the trees* (LXX τοῦ ξύλου) of the garden.' Notice the uses of the tenses in 2 Tim. i. 8, ii. 1-3, iv. 2, 5 νῆφε ... ἔργον ποίησον εὐαγγελιστοῦ κ.τ.λ.

Logion V

4.

Understanding the injunction to raise up the stone and cleave the tree literally, and paraphrasing it by words of Jesus in the apocryphal Gospel of Thomas (A. xviii ποίει τὸ ἔργον σου), we may say that the Logion means '*Do thy work*, and I will be with thee.'

To this it may be objected, that such sayings of our Lord are not to be found in the canonical Scriptures. 'To say, as some may feel disposed to say, "The general drift is clear; it means that Jesus promised to be present with the mason and the carpenter, and (by implication) with every disciple engaged in his ordinary occupation," is simply to give up all prospect of honestly entering into the Lord's meaning. For when did the Lord ever make such a promise? How, indeed, could He make it to men whom He was sending forth to convert the world, and urging to give all their energies to sowing the seed of the Gospel and to plowing its fields, or to shepherding the flock and bringing back the lost sheep, or to labouring in the vineyard by digging and gathering out the stones and cutting down the trees and rooting up the weeds and erecting a tower and planting and pruning the vines?' Such words as 'sowing,' 'planting,' 'cutting down,' 'rooting up' were always used by Jesus metaphorically, and He 'could not (so far as we can judge) have used them in a literal sense.' Hence it might be concluded, either that, because (B) is a genuine Logion, it is not to be understood literally; or that, because it should apparently be so understood, it is not genuine.

In the canonical saying most akin to it there is no such metaphorical language, and no reference to missionary work. It is merely said in plain words, that if two disciples agree in prayer, the Father in heaven will hearken, for where two or three are gathered together in His name there will Jesus be in the midst of them. Even if He had promised His presence in express words only to preachers of the Gospel, something like the saying (B), literally interpreted, must sooner or later have been read into His words; for, as time went on and Christians multiplied, it would have become more and more apparent that all could not be actively employed in converting the nations to the faith.

(A) *and* (B).

It remains to consider another interpretation of οὐκ ἄθεοι in (A), and the relation of (A) and (B) to one another.

1.

OYK EICIN AΘEOI
EΓW EIMI MET AYTOY.

Some restorers of Logion V make the persons spoken of at its commencement 'godless,' and some make them 'not godless' (L. S. p. 11). The expression, 'not without God,' may have been a natural one in the original surroundings from which the Logion has been cut away, but it is hard to fix its most probable exact connotation now. The peculiarity of the phrase, which has not been much dwelt upon, may be shewn by the suggestion of contexts in which it would be not inappropriate.

(1) On the hypothesis of a contrast with larger numbers than two, as in sayings quoted from Pirké Aboth, it might be said, שְׁנַיִם אֵינָם בְּלֹא שְׁכִינָה, *Two—they are not without Shechinah;* and then, *Even one—Shechinah is with him.* So in the Logion Jesus might be thought to say, 'Only two are not godless; and I am with even one.'

(2) With 1 Cor. xi. 11, 'Nevertheless neither is the man without the woman, neither the woman without the man, in the Lord,' compare the saying quoted from the Midrash in *Sayings of the Jewish Fathers,* chap. i, note 12, lit. *Not man without woman, and not woman without man, and not both of them without Shechinah*—the two together are not godless. An Oxyrhynchus, with its many monks and virgins, may have read into the Logion, whatever was its true sense, a contrast between the married and the single; allowing the two to be 'not godless,' but setting them

Logion V

at a lower spiritual level than the one. Professor Lock ends his comments upon Logion V (A) thus, 'The meaning of this will be, "where there are a few Christians or only one," and the application may have been primarily either to common or private prayer, or perhaps to married or celibate life,' comparing Clem. Alex. *Strom.* iii. 10 (L. S. pp. 11, 23).

Professor J. A. Robinson in the *Expositor* (vol. vi. 5th series, 1897) writes of this remarkable passage of the *Stromateis*, that 'Clement of Alexandria is defending Holy Matrimony against impugners of two kinds ... It is with the error on the side of asceticism that we shall be here concerned, and we must pick out the main passages which deal with it,' and continues on *Strom.* iii:—

'§ 1. The followers of Basilides use Matthew xix. 10–12 (*eunuchs for the kingdom of heaven's sake*). In refuting their view, Clement says (§ 4): ἡμεῖς εὐνουχίαν μὲν καὶ οἷς τοῦτο δεδώρηται ὑπὸ θεοῦ μακαρίζομεν ... The word μακαρίζομεν in this connexion is to be noted.'

'§ 45. The extreme ascetics cite a conversation of our Lord with Salome: the answer to the question, *How long shall death prevail?* is this: *As long as ye women bring forth children.* The source of the citation is not here stated. Clement explains the words to mean: As long as the present order lasts, in which as the sequence of nature γένεσις is followed by φθορά.'

'In §§ 63–67 he returns to the passage about Salome, and says: φέρεται δέ, οἶμαι, ἐν τῷ κατ' Αἰγυπτίους εὐαγγελίῳ,' he opines that it is in the Gospel according to the Egyptians.

'Then in § 68 he suddenly asks: *But who are the two and three gathered in the name of Christ, among whom the Lord is in the midst?* He suggests various answers. In the first place he says: *Is it not husband and wife and child that he means by the three?* for "to husband wife is joined by God" (Prov. xix. 14, LXX). A similar interpretation of the preceding verse (Matt. xviii. 19, *If two of you shall agree*) is mentioned by Origen as propounded by one of his predecessors (*Comm. in Matth.*, t. 14, c. 2; *Ru.* iii. 617).'

'The heretics with whom Clement is dealing interpret the meaning of Christ to be, that *with the many is the* DEMIURGE, *the God of* genesis, *but with the one, the elect, is the* SAVIOUR, *who is Son of another God, to wit, the good God,*' cf. L. S. pp. 11-12. Clement replies that the same God, through the Son, is (as we may say) with the '*two.*'

'He then suggests alternative interpretations of "the three," such as θυμός, ἐπιθυμία, and λογισμός; or, again, σάρξ, ψυχή, and πνεῦμα. Stress appears to be laid on the "gathering together," the union of the τριάς, as he calls it, whatever its component parts may be interpreted to be.'

'He is still struggling with the interpretation in § 70, where he suggests a new possibility : " Or perhaps with *the one*, the Jew, the Lord was in giving the law ; but in prophesying and sending Jeremiah to Babylon, and yet further in calling those of the Gentiles through prophecy, he was gathering peoples (who were) *the two ;* and *a third* was being created out of the two unto a new man, in whom indeed He walks and dwells, to wit, in the Church.' See Eph. ii. 14-15, 'who hath made both one ... that he might create in himself of the twain one new man.'

In § 91 he quotes from Julius Cassianus Περὶ ἐγκρατείας ἢ περὶ εὐνουχίας, '... He would not have *pronounced* the eunuchs *blessed* (ἐμακάρισεν), nor would the prophet have said that they were *not a fruitless tree* (Isaiah lvi).'

In §§ 92-93 he mentions Cassianus as having quoted words of the Lord to Salome, which were not in one of the Four Gospels, but only in the Gospel according to the Egyptians. To Cassianus probably 'Clement has been referring in the earlier sections.'

In §§ 98-99 he sums up the controversy by spiritualizing the eunuch of Isaiah lvi and his sabbath-keeping, ending thus : But they that *have eunuchized themselves from all sin for the kingdom of heaven's sake, these are blessed— they that fast from the world.*

Before the discovery of the Oxyrhynchus Logia it would

have been very hard to account for some things in this passage of the *Stromateis*. Logion V now supplies an explanation of the contrast between the Demiurge and the Saviour, who are with the two and the one respectively, by teaching that the 'two' are not godless, but Jesus is with the 'one alone.' Although Clement does not quote the saying, something like it seems to lie at the root of the discussion.

In a note on chap. xi of the *Ancient Homily* of pseudo-Clement of Rome, Bishop Lightfoot writes:—

'ὑπό τινος] By Salome. This incident was reported in the Gospel of the Egyptians, as we learn from Clem. Alex. *Strom*. iii. 13, p. 533 (in a passage quoted from Julius Cassianus) . . . Similar passages from this gospel and apparently from the same context are quoted by Clement previously . . . There is nothing in these passages to suggest that Clement himself had read this gospel (unless, indeed, as has occurred to me, we should read τί δὲ οὐχὶ κ.τ.λ.; for τί δέ; οὐχὶ κ.τ.λ. in *Strom*. iii. 9), and the expressions λέγουσι, οἶμαι, φασί, seem to imply the contrary; though it is generally assumed that he was acquainted with it.'

2.

The Logion is made up of (A), 'Wheresoever there be two . . . and where there is one only &c.,' and (B), 'Raise thou the stone &c.' The statement (A) may be classed with a group of Christian and other sayings, of which examples have been given: the saying (B), which is unique in character and in the form of an address, may be assumed to be an addition to (A), of which there are traces elsewhere without it. But (B) having been appended to (A) by the Logiographer, we have to choose between contrasting the two parts of the Logion and interpreting them together as a continuous whole.

(1) The pantheistic interpretation of (B) contrasts the two members of the Logion, making the presence of Jesus in the one of a different order from His presence in the

other—a presence in stocks and stones in (B), as against a presence with persons in (A). Nor does it give any special significance to the singulars, 'Raise *thou* the stone ... cleave *thou* the tree.'

(2) To make the whole saying continuous, we must make (B) teach something of distinctive interest to εἷς μόνος, the one alone. To do this we may suppose the Lord, after saying that He will be with the one, to change to the direct form of address and say in effect that He will be with the solitary Christian at his work, whatever that may be. This work may be understood to be spiritual or secular. If spiritual, according to one view it is spiritual *building*. Supposing the two and the one to be the married and the single, we may then compare Isaiah lvi. 4–5, 'For thus saith the Lord unto the eunuchs that keep my sabbaths ... Even unto them will I give in mine house and within my walls a place and a name better than of sons and daughters.' The one alone may take his part in raising up the spiritual house.

If the work be taken to be a typical form of manual labour, the sense will be that Jesus is present with the disciple who is, by force of circumstances, cut off from the congregation, and from directly religious occupations and service. Thus the saying would strikingly supplement His assurances of His presence with those engaged in preaching His Gospel or assembled in His name, while giving the closest connexion between the second part of the Logion and the words next before it in the first part.

In Ecclus. vii. 15, 'Hate not laborious work; Neither husbandry, which the Most High hath ordained,' passing over the express mention of *husbandry* as perhaps not belonging to the original work, we have a general precept to the effect, 'Do thy work, for it is thy portion from God,' which forms a good parallel to Logion V (B) taken literally.

Compare the rabbinic saying * in commendation of labour,

---

* See the Midrash on Jacob's Well for interpretations of the STONE upon the well's mouth (*Jewish Fathers*, Addit. Note 16), and compare Deut. Rab. vi *fin.*, quoted in Schoettgen *Hor. Heb.* ii. 67 (Dresd. & Lips. 1742). In

Logion V 53

that 'The Shechinah was not to dwell with Israel till they had made a sanctuary (Exod. xxv. 8). "Six days *must* (not *mayest*) thou labour, and do all thy work:" labour if poor, but find "work" to do even if rich' (*Jewish Fathers*, i. n. 22).

(3) It is possible to combine an allusion to the pantheistic doctrine with the strictly literal view of (B). St. Paul can quote words of heathen poets, as Aratus and Cleanthes (Acts xvii. 28–29), without going on to say that 'the Godhead is found in gold, silver and stone,' and pervades all things, even to the meanest and most disgusting *. So Jesus in the Logion may be thought to teach that even the anchoret, working in solitude among stones and trees, will *find* Him, not in the sense that the Stoic 'God,' the mind of the world, is everywhere ἐν τῇ ὕλῃ, in matter, but in the religious sense of Exod. xx. 24, 'In every place ... I will come unto thee.' 'Why is God called MAKOM?' that is, *place* (τόπος). 'Because "in every place" where the righteous stand He is found' (*Yalkut*, i. 119).

Early expounders of (B) may have departed from its true sense and allegorized what they should have taken literally, as the manual work which Jesus 'the carpenter' (Mark vi. 3) is said to have done was made to have a spiritual significance. In Justin's *Trypho* (§ 88, Otto, p. 324) our Lord is said to have made *ploughs and yokes*, by these as symbols teaching righteousness and the duties of active life (Matt. xi. 29; Luke ix. 62). What He did must have been a sign: what He is reported to have said must have been a parable.

Hermas (*Sim.* ix. 9. 7) the Tower when finished was 'as if of one stone,' μονόλιθος γάρ μοι ἐδόκει εἶναι. So Jacob at Haran took 'of the stones' of the place, and in the morning found them 'the stone' (Gen. xxviii. 11, 18), for (*Yalkut*, i. 119) נעשו כל אבן אחה, they had all of them been made one stone.

* Zeller, *Philos. der Griechen*, 3ter Theil, i. § 4 (p. 126, 1865), 'das Schlechteste und Hässlichste so gut wie das Schönste,' with footnote including the illustrations from Clem. Alex. and Lucian given above on page 39.

VI

LOGION VI.

Λέγει 'Ιησοῦς,
(A) Οὐκ ἔστιν δεκτὸς προφήτης ἐν τῇ πατρίδι αὐτοῦ.
(B) Οὐδὲ ἰατρὸς ποιεῖ θεραπείας εἰς τοὺς γινώσκοντας αὐτόν.

Saith Jesus,
A prophet is not acceptable in his own country, neither doth a physician work cures upon them that know him.

The parallels in the Gospels are:—

St. Matt. xiii. 57-58: 'And they were offended in him. But Jesus said unto them, A prophet is not without honour, save in his own country, and in his own house. And he did not many mighty works there because of their unbelief.'

St. Mark vi. 4-5: 'And Jesus said unto them, A prophet is not without honour, save in his own country, and among his own kin, and in his own house. And he could there do no mighty work, save that he laid his hands upon a few sick folk, and healed them. And he marvelled because of their unbelief.'

St. Luke iv. 23-24: 'And he said unto them, Doubtless ye will say unto me this parable, Physician, heal thyself: whatsoever we have heard done at Capernaum, do also here in thine own country. And he said, Verily I say unto you, No prophet is acceptable in his own country.'

St. John iv. 44: 'For Jesus himself testified, that a prophet hath no honour in his own country.'

(A)

Comparing the first saying in the Logion with the following parallels from the first and second, the third, and the fourth Gospels respectively:—

(1) Οὐκ ἔστιν προφήτης ἄτιμος εἰ μὴ ἐν τῇ πατρίδι αὐτοῦ,
(2) Οὐδεὶς προφήτης δεκτός ἐστιν ἐν τῇ πατρίδι αὐτοῦ,
(3) Προφήτης ἐν τῇ ἰδίᾳ πατρίδι τιμὴν οὐκ ἔχει,

Logion VI

we see that it might have been drawn from (1) and (2) with or without (3), that is to say, from the three Synoptic Gospels, with or without the Fourth Gospel. Inserting δεκτός from (2) before προφήτης in (1), and omitting ἄτιμος εἰ μή, we get the saying (A).

(B)

'The second part of this *logion* is new' (Swete), but not in its obvious sense true. ' No one can assert that a physician, in the literal sense, "does not work cures on them that know him." Jesus is therefore manifestly speaking of a physician of the soul and of nothing but spiritual healing. In this sense, familiarity with the healer is well known as an impediment to the act of healing. The synoptists hint at it in various ways ... But it is reserved for John to represent the Jews as saying directly that they cannot believe in any Messiah whose origin they "know," and Jesus as replying in two apparently inconsistent statements, " Ye both *know* me and know whence I am," and again, " Ye *know* neither me nor my Father." The meaning of both is obvious ... The prophet is " known," and yet "not known," by the neighbours whom he cannot heal because they cannot believe' (Abbott, p. 23).

The Gospels record that Jesus in His own country could not, or did not, do many works of healing, as He did in places where He was not so well known.

Wetstein on St. Luke, loc. cit., quotes from Dio Chrysostom, ὅστις δὲ ὀκνεῖ τὴν ἑαυτοῦ πόλιν ἑκοῦσαν καὶ ἐπικαλουμένην διοικεῖν, ὅμοιός ἐστιν ὥσπερ εἴ τις τὸ μὲν ἑαυτοῦ σῶμα θεραπεύειν μὴ θέλοι, ἀξιῶν ἰατρὸς εἶναι, ἄλλους ʼδὲ ἀνθρώπους ἰατρεύοι κ.τ.λ., a man who will not answer the call to take part in the administration of his own city is like a physician who does not choose to attend to his own body, but will heal others for a fee. Thus the case of a man who will not be at the trouble of, so far as in him lies, regulating and reforming a body corporate to which he belongs is likened to the hypothetical case of a physician who will not heal himself.

According to St. Luke, our Lord supposes an analogous application of the proverb, 'Physician, heal thyself,'—'*exert thy powers of healing in thine own country*, as presently interpreted; the Physician being represented as an inhabitant of Nazareth, and σεαυτόν including His own citizens in it' (Alford). In the Gospel the proverb and its application are put by Him into the mouth of others, thus, 'And he said unto them, Doubtless ye will say unto me this parable, Physician, heal thyself: whatsoever we have heard done at Capernaum, do also here in thine own country.' Then follows the first saying in the Logion in the form, '*Verily I say unto you, No prophet is acceptable in his own country*,' with a λέγω of Jesus corresponding to the Logiographer's λέγει Ἰησοῦς.

Unbelieving neighbours at Nazareth having been made to say implicitly, 'Thou, a physician, dost not do cures to them that know thee,' in order to deduce therefrom the second part of the Logion, we must generalize their saying about Jesus and make it His. A like handling of the words quoted from Dio Chrysostom would lead to another new proverb, as untrue generally as what is new to us in the Logion appears on the face of it to be.

In passages cited by Wetstein from Aeschylus, Cicero, and other writers, the physician who cannot heal himself is assumed to be a bad one (κακός, *malus*). But in the following illustrations from Aristotle (vols. ii. 40, x. 91 in Bekker, Oxon. 1837), a man's healing or not healing himself is regarded from different points of view:—

(1) Phys. 2. 8, 199 b 30: ὥστ' εἰ ἐν τῇ τέχνῃ ἔνεστι τὸ ἕνεκά του, κἀὶ ἐν φύσει. μάλιστα δὲ δῆλον, ὅταν τις ἰατρεύῃ αὐτὸς ἑαυτόν· τούτῳ γὰρ ἔοικεν ἡ φύσις.

(2) Pol. 3. 16, 1287 a 41: ἀλλὰ μὴν εἰσάγονταί γ' ἐφ' ἑαυτοὺς οἱ ἰατροὶ κάμνοντες ἄλλους ἰατροὺς καὶ οἱ παιδοτρίβαι γυμναζόμενοι παιδοτρίβας, ὡς οὐ δυνάμενοι κρίνειν τὸ ἀληθὲς διὰ τὸ κρίνειν περί τε οἰκείων καὶ ἐν πάθει ὄντες.

Aristotle in (1) is arguing that there is a 'wherefore' or

purpose in nature: he supposes the case of a man who acts as his own physician, and says that nature does likewise.

In (2) he states that physicians and gymnastic trainers are accustomed, for good reasons, to call in others for their own healing or training. A man cannot always judge rightly about what concerns himself, and his faculties may be impaired by a disease from which he is suffering.

For a like reason to the former, in cases of difficulty a physician may quite naturally call in other physicians to treat those whom *he knows* best, that is to say, the members of his own family. It also happens sometimes that a physician has not the opportunity of healing 'them that know him,' merely because they have no faith in one with whom they are familiarly acquainted. But it is not true generally that a physician of bodies does not heal his neighbours. The saying (B) is nearer the truth when taken spiritually, and as a doublet of (A).

ποιεῖ θεραπείας] For the phrase see *Protevang. Jac.* xx.

εἰς τοὺς γινώσκοντας αὐτόν] Cf. in Psalm lxxxvi. 4 τοῖς γινώσκουσί με. 'Have we not here a trace of the Aramaic origin of the *logion*?' (Swete, p. 548).

VII.

LOGION VII.

Λέγει Ἰησοῦς,

Πόλις ᾠκοδομημένη ἐπ᾽ ἄκρον ὄρους ὑψηλοῦ καὶ ἐστηριγμένη οὔτε πεσεῖν δύναται οὔτε κρυβῆναι.

Saith Jesus,

A city built on the top of a high hill and stablished can neither fall nor be hid.

The Logion gives the substance of two sayings from the Sermon on the Mount, but with variations which have to be accounted for. The two sayings, as nearly as may be in the words of the Logion, are:—

(A) *A city on the top of a high hill cannot be hid.*
(B) *A city built and stablished cannot fall.*

(A)

ἐπ' ἄκρον ὄρους ὑψηλοῦ] Our Lord having said, according to St. Matthew (v. 14), 'A city set on *a hill* cannot be hid,' why does the Logion speak of the city as built upon *the top of a high hill*? In so concise a saying, with its abbreviation and compression, it is not likely that a *hill* has been expanded into the *top of a high hill* without purpose and significance. An adequate explanation seems to be suggested by the following passage from *The Witness of Hermas to the Four Gospels* (p. 25 sq., 1892):—

'In Sim. ix we read, And he took me away to Arcadia, unto a certain rounded mountain, and set me on the top of the mountain; and he shewed me a great plain, and round about the plain twelve mountains (1. 4). And in the midst of the plain he shewed me a great white rock rising up out of the plain: the rock was higher than the mountains, four-square, so that it could contain the whole world (2. 1). On the rock, above a gate hewn out of it, a tower is built of stones brought from all the mountains (4. 2, 5), in the last days (12. 3). The tower is the Church (13. 1). The rock on which it is built is therefore the mountain of the Lord's house; and its being higher than the mountains alludes to the saying of Micah iv. 1 and Isaiah ii. 2, *And it shall come to pass in the last days, that the mountain of the Lord's house shall be established in the top of the mountains, and shall be exalted above the hills; and all nations shall flow unto it.*' With allusion, we may suppose, to this famous prediction of two prophets, the city in the Logion is built and established 'on the top of a high hill.'

The twelve mountains in the *Shepherd* being twelve tribes 'that inhabit the whole world' (17. 1), the mountain from which they are all seen recalls the mountain of the Temptation (Matt. iv. 8). The Logion possibly alludes also to this, and to other texts such as Ezek. xx. 40, xxxiv. 14, xl. 2, '... a very high mountain, whereon was as it were the frame of a city.'

Logion VII

A city set (κειμένη) *on a hill**. Compare the following uses of the word for SET:—

Rev. xxi. 16: 'And the city *lieth* foursquare.'

Ecclus. xxii. 16-18: 'Timber girt and bound into a *building* shall not be loosed with shaking: So a heart *established* (ἐστηριγμένη) in due season on well advised counsel shall not be afraid . . . Pales *set* on a high place will not stand against the wind.'

Hermas *Vis*. iii., *Sim*. ix. (*Witness of Hermas*, p. 45): '. . . stones rejected by the builders. Many such stones are seen in *Vis*. iii. *lying* about the tower, seamed, stunted, or otherwise unfit for use (2. 8) . . . In *Sim*. ix. the stones *lying* by the tower are given over to the Shepherd to cleanse, and he says that he will hew most of them, and cast them into the building.' See also the suggestive article on the *Logia* by Mr. Charles B. Huleatt in No. 2723 of the *Guardian* (Feb. 9, 1898).

The word for SET in the Sermon on the Mount (Matt. v. 14) perfectly suits its context; but some word connoting stability, which 'set' does not, was wanted in the Logion.

(B)

St. Matt. vii. 24-25: 'Every one therefore which heareth these words of mine, and doeth them, shall be likened unto a wise man, which built his house upon the rock: and the rain descended, and the floods came, and the winds blew, and beat upon that house; and it fell not: for it was founded upon the rock.'

St. Luke vi. 47-49: 'I will shew you to whom he is like: he is like a man building a house, who digged and went deep, and laid a foundation upon the rock: and when a flood arose, the stream brake against that house, and could not shake it: *because it had been well builded*.' So the Revised Version, with the note, 'Many ancient authori-

---

* *Ye are the light of the world. A city &c.* (Matt. v. 14). Compare Wetstein's illustration from Cicero, *Catilin.* iv. 6: 'Video enim mihi hanc urbem videre, lucem orbis terrarum atque arcem omnium gentium.'

tics read *for it had been founded upon the rock*: as in Matt. vii. 25.' Dr. Gifford quotes from Tisch.-Baljon *N. T. Gr.* 1898, on St. Luke, 'aeth. *quia supra petram aedificata fuit ac bene aedificata fuit.*' *Built*, MS. οἰκοδομημένη (Swete, p. 549)] The use of *built* for *set* (Matt. v. 14) in the Logion may be accounted for by supposing it to rest upon some form or version of the Sermon on the Mount in which the word *built* was so used. '*A city built on the top of a high hill and firmly stablished can neither fall nor be hidden.* This combines the thought of St. Matt. v. 14 with that of vii. 24, 25, but does not compel the theory of literary dependence. The word οἰκοδομημένη (St. Matt. v. 14 κειμένη) is interesting, for though not found in any Greek MS. of the passage in St. Matthew, it seems to be presupposed by the early Syriac versions, by Tatian, and by a Latin version used by Hilary' (L. S. p. 26).

As a simple alternative to this explanation it may be suggested that the word *built* in the Logion alludes to the parable of the House on the Rock, in which the word 'build' is used. This word suits both of the sayings combined in the Logion, whereas 'set' applies only to the position of the city and not to its structure. The word as being so appropriate in the Logion might have been thought of merely as a synonym for 'set'; but its occurrence in the parable may actually have suggested it.

Stablished] Professor Swete writes, 'I am unable to see the force of the argument which the editors urge against the hypothesis of conflation, on the ground that there is no reference to the rock. The rock is implied in ἐστηριγμένη. The saying is, however, not so much a conflation as an abbreviation, which labours to collect the ideas of two very distinct sayings, and produces in its present detached form a somewhat confused result ... στηρίζειν, which occurs in Luke, Cath., Paul, Apoc., is not used in the New Testament or apparently in the LXX of the foundation of a building, for which Matthew has the proper word θεμελιοῦν.' But 'stablished' means more than 'founded':

Logion VII

an edifice which is to stand must be not merely on a good foundation, but also 'well builded.' 'For other foundation can no man lay than that which is laid, which is Jesus Christ. But if any man buildeth on the foundation gold, silver, costly stones, wood, hay, stubble; each man's work shall be manifest: for the day shall declare it' (1 Cor. iii. 11-13).

Fall] Rev. xi. 13: 'And in that hour there was a great earthquake, and the tenth part of the city fell.' Rev. xvi. 18-19: 'And there was a great earthquake, such as was not since there were men upon the earth, so great an earthquake, so mighty. And the great city was divided into three parts, and the cities of the nations fell.' A city or more or less of it may be thrown down by an earthquake; but that an entire city should fall, as a single house might do, because it is not well built would be an extraordinary occurrence (Harnack). Why should so strange a thing be contemplated in the Logion? The theory of conflation is required to account for it. The Logion compresses widely different sayings about a *city* and a *house* into one: for the sake of brevity it makes the one word serve for both: and thus it applies to a city what in one of the sayings relates to a house.

Dr. Abbott comments thus on the Logion, 'The next Logion combines two sayings from the Sermon on the Mount . . . It warns the Christian teacher, first, that he is to teach, and, secondly, that he is to know. Publicity is to be accompanied with certainty. The tower is to be high, but it is also to have firm foundations. The two thoughts go well together in this antithesis, and their harmony indicates that we have here an original saying of Jesus, or of some early inspired follower of Jesus, and not a mere scribal combination of two sayings. And there is a passage of Clement of Alexandria, similarly connecting the notions of "height" and "stablishing," which makes it probable that this Logion was in some shape known to him. Quoting the Psalmist's precept to "tell the towers of Jerusalem," he says: "This suggests that those who in a *high spirit* (ὑψηλῶς) have received the word [of God] will be like *high towers* and will stand *firmly* in faith and knowledge."'

The Logiographer, in making the one word 'city' serve, not very appropriately, for both 'city' and 'house,' was doubtless thinking again of little but spiritual applications. The *city* was the Church, which was also a *house*. It was the city 'which hath foundations,' and was *built* upon the rock, Christ. The Church was 'as a city built on a height' (*Clem. Hom.* iii. 67, in Resch *Paralleltexte*). It was like Jerusalem, which was 'builded as a city &c.' (Ps. cxxii. 3).

A commentator on *Civitas super montem posita,* 'a city set on a hill,' when he says that the 'city' is the Church, instinctively goes on to paraphrase 'set' by *built*. Thus Theophilus in *Allegor.* lib. i. 5 writes, '*Civitas* ecclesia, *mons* intelligendus est Christus, super quem *aedificata est ecclesia*' (Zahn, *Forsch.*). The Logiographer, to whom the 'city' was the Church, would in like manner quite naturally have spoken of it as 'built,' a word which suited both the sayings which he was welding together, and was actually used in one of them.

VIII

LOGION VIII.

ΛΕΓΕΙ ΙC ΑΚΟΥΕΙC
[·]ΙCΤΟΕ̣ . . ΤΙΟΝ COY ΤΟ̣

1.

Thou hearest into thy one ear.

The note upon Logion VIII in G. H. (p. 15) is as follows:—
'As at the bottom of col. 1, the traces of letters in the middle of l. 42 are very faint. The third letter could be Γ, the fifth C. [Ε]ΙC ΤΟ ΕΝѠΠΙΟΝ COY is a possible reading. The last letter of the line may be Ε, and the preceding one Γ or conceivably Κ. The Logion appears to be new.'

Logion VIII

Filling the three blanks in line 42 with the letters Є, N, Ѡ, suggested in this note, we get for the beginning of the saying,

ΑΚΟΥΕΙC ΕΙCΤΟΕΝѠΤΙΟΝ COY.

The obvious way of reading ΕΙCΤΟΕΝѠΤΙΟΝ is given in the note of L. S. (p. 14) on the text of the Logion, 'εἰς τὸ ἐν ὠτίον (Taylor *ap*. Swete, Zahn, v. Gebhardt).' Professor Swete writes (p. 549 n.) that he owes the suggestion of ὠτίον to the present writer: he had himself 'thought of ἐνώτιον = οὖς': and he continues the saying on hearing 'with one ear' with words meaning, 'but the other thou hast closed,' the closing of one ear being supposed to imply hearing indistinctly. Messrs. Grenfell and Hunt, to whom the reading ἐν ὠτίον properly belongs, write in *The Oxyrhynchus Papyri*:—

'Alone of restorations Swete's ἀκούεις [ε]ἰς τὸ ἐν ὠτίον σοῦ τὸ [δὲ ἕτερον συνέκλεισας (or some such word) in the eighth Saying is quite convincing. The sense is, "Thou hearest with one ear, but the other thou hast closed," i.e. "thou attendest imperfectly to my message."'

2.

Aure dextra intende.

Hearing εἰς τὸ ἐν ὠτίον, 'with the one ear,' suggested to me something different from hearing indistinctly or with inattention.

(1) In the Bible and elsewhere the 'right' takes precedence of the 'left.' Compare the following and other places of the Old and New Testaments in which mention is made of the right ear or other member:—

Exod. xxix. 20 (Lev. viii. 23-24, xiv. 14-28): 'Then shalt thou kill the ram, and take of his blood, and put it upon the tip of the right ear of Aaron, and upon the tip of the right ear of his sons, and upon the thumb of their right hand, and upon the thumb (*anglice* great toe) of their right foot, and sprinkle the blood upon the altar round about.'

Zech. xi. 17: 'Woe to the idol shepherd that leaveth the

flock! the sword shall be upon his arm, and upon his right eye: his arm shall be clean dried up, and his right eye shall be utterly darkened.'

St. Matt. v. 29-30: 'And if thy right eye offend thee, pluck it out ... And if thy right hand offend thee, cut it off, and cast it from thee.'

St. Matt. vi. 3: '... let not thy left hand know what thy right hand doeth.'

St. John for some reason mentions (xviii. 10) that it was the right ear of Malchus that was cut off. The net (xxi. 6) was to be cast on the right side.

(2) The Midrash makes YAD, *hand*, mean the left hand, as in Isa. xlviii. 13: 'Mine hand also hath laid the foundation of the earth, and my right hand hath spanned the heavens.' The left hand created earth, and the right hand heaven. See *Sayings of the Jewish Fathers*, chap. v, note 40 (cf. ii. n. 17), and Clem. *Hom.* ii. 16, quoted at the end of chap. ii (ed. 2, 1897): 'In beginning* God, being One, as things right and left first made the heaven, then the earth; and so consecutively all the syzygies.'

(3) Exod. xxi. 6: '... and his master shall bore *his ear* through with an aul; and he shall serve him for ever,' Targ. 'Jonathan' ית אודניה ימינא, *his right ear*. The Mechilta (Friedmann, f. 77 a, Weiss, p. 84) makes out by a *g'zerah shavah*, or (as we may say) argument *ex aequali*, that 'his ear' means his right ear. See Talmud Babli *Zebaḥim* 24 a sq. for a disputed *g'zerah shavah*, on the question of the right hand as the hand for giving and receiving, comparing St. Matt. vi. 3 quoted above.

The Mechilta raises the question, Why was the ear, of all members, to be bored? It was because the ear heard the Commandments from Sinai.

(4) Eccles. i. 16: 'I spake with my heart, saying ...' The heart therefore hears. The Midrash on the words cited

---

* The first word of the Bible (written in MSS. without vowels) is traditionally read as pointed *B'reshith*, i.e. without the article, and is rendered accordingly in the Septuagint and the Fourth Gospel. Rabbinic writers note that the word is not to be read, *Bareshith*, in *the* beginning.

Logion VIII

ascribes a number of actions and faculties to the heart, including *hearing*, for which the Scripture proof is 1 Kings iii. 9 לב שמע, *a hearing heart*; and *receiving commandments*, for which the proof is Prov. x. 8 'חכם לב כו.

Eccles. x. 2: 'A wise man's heart is at his right hand; but a fool's heart at his left.' The Yalkut applies this verse to the righteous, who meditate on the Torah, which was given with the right hand; and the wicked, who give their heart to grow rich, for it is said (Prov. iii. 16), 'in her left hand riches and honour.'

(5) For the following apt illustration, from a work attributed to Philo, I am indebted to Dr. Rendel Harris. The passage is taken from a volume entitled ΜΙΚΡΟ-ΠΡΕΣΒΥΤΙΚΟΝ (Basil., date at end of pref. Kal. Sept. MDL), which contains *inter alia*, 'PHILONIS JUDAEI *Antiquitatum Biblicarum liber incerto interprete.*'

See page 334*, where in the margin is written, *Dextra aure audire Deum*, of hearing God with the right ear; and in the text Eli tells the child Samuel to listen with his right ear, and not with the left; because Phinehas the priest taught that the right ear hears the Lord by night, and the left an angel:—

'Aure tua dextra intende, sinistra tace. Phinees enim sacerdos praecepit nobis dicens: Auris dextra audit dominum per noctem, sinistra autem angelum. Et ideo si in dextra audieris, dicito: Dic quid uis, quoniam audio, tu enim me plasmasti. Si autem in sinistra audieris, ueni & annuntia mihi.'

Samuel goes away and sleeps: the Lord speaks again, *& repleta est Samueli dextra auris:* then he turns on to the other side and says, 'Si possibilis sum, loquere . . .'

---

* The passage from 'Philonis Ant. Bibl.' is on p. 94 in the Basel reprint of 1538 from the *editio princeps* (Basel, 1527). The reprint has on its title-page, 'Philonis Judaei Alexandrini . . . omnes *quae* apud Graecos et Latinos extant, libri, Antiquitatum . . .' (I. B.).

3.
The Two Ways.

The doctrine of the *Two Ways* appears in a multitude of forms in sacred and profane literature.

Justin, *Apol.* ii. 11, quotes the myth of Prodicus on the *Choice of Hercules* from Xenophon, in which Virtue and Vice appear as women, and address Hercules at the dividing of the ways. In the *Testaments of the Twelve Patriarchs* (Jud. 20) we read: 'Two spirits wait upon a man, that of truth and that of error (1 John iv. 6), and between is that of the understanding of the mind, whichsoever way it may will to incline.'

The supposed hearing 'into the one ear' in Logion VIII suggested to me a form of the *Two Ways* in which the man might be imagined to be solicited by voices without forms, as it is said in Isa. xxx. 21: 'And thine ears shall hear a word behind thee, saying, This is the way, walk ye in it, when ye turn to the right hand, and when ye turn to the left.'

Ways themselves are personified and speak in Herodotus, as noted by Diels (I. B.) in *Parmenides' Lehrgedicht*, p. 47 (Berlin, 1897), with the remark: 'Dieser Tropus erklärt die Worte des vierten Evangeliums . . . ἐγὼ εἰμὶ ἡ ὁδός . . .'. In Herod. ii. 20-22 three Greek *ways* of accounting for the overflow of the Nile are specified; and first two are noticed, τῶν ἡ ἑτέρα λέγει, *whereof the one says* that the Etesian winds are the cause, and *the other* is ἀνεπιστημονεστέρη, more unintelligent. But 'the third of the ways, though far most reasonable, does most speak false (ἔψευσται), for neither does this say (λέγει) anything when it says (φαμένη) that the Nile flows from melting snow.'

Whether or not the Logion was on the subject of two opposing voices speaking into the right ear and the left respectively, or in any sense upon τὸ ἓν ὠτίον, it has served to call attention to some curious sayings, and may in due time be the means of bringing others of equal or greater interest to light.

IX

CONCLUSION.

THIS concluding section contains additional notes on some of the Oxyrhynchus Sayings, and touches upon the general questions of their use by early Christian writers, and the sources, nature, and purpose of the Logiographer's compilation. The proposed new reading in Logion II (p. 7 n.), which is Mr. V. P. Bartlet's, is 'Jesus,' for 'God.'

1.

The Kingdom of Jesus.

The phrase 'kingdom of Jesus' is found in the *Epistle of Barnabas* (p. 72), and is led up to by passages of the New Testament :—

St. John xviii. 36 : 'Jesus answered, My kingdom is not of this world.' Thus the new reading would not impair the parallelism, ' world,' ' kingdom . . . ,' in Logion II (A).

St. Luke xxiii. 42 (Matt. xx. 21): 'And he said, Jesus, remember me when thou comest in thy kingdom.'

St. Luke i. 31–33 (Matt. xiii. 41, xvi. 28): '. . . and thou shalt call his name Jesus . . . and of his kingdom there shall be no end.'

Rev. i. 9 (Col. i. 11–13): '. . . the tribulation and kingdom and patience in Jesus.'

Having learned from Dr. Rendel Harris that the reading ΘΥ (θεοῦ) in Logion II had been called in question, and that it had been proposed to alter it in some way, I examined the facsimile, and invited others to examine it, with the following results.

1. Some thought of OYI.OY, or OYNOY, a contraction for οὐρανοῦ, *of heaven*. One correspondent wrote at first, 'I see that the space seems large for ΘΥ : can it be OYNOY? But I think that hardly likely. TOY is clear ' ; and afterwards suggested 'TOYNOY written for TOYOYNOY by homoio-

teleuton,' with the remark, 'considering the smallness of the O in this script, there seems to be room, as far as one can judge from the facsimile.' These readings are testimony against ΘΥ, and in favour of a stroke Ι next after ΤΟΥ, which might be either an *iota* or part of a larger letter as Ν or Κ. There is room for ΚΥ (cf. 2 Pet. i. 11 βασιλείαν τοῦ Κυρίου, κ.τ.λ.), but scarcely for ΝΟΥ.

2. The Ι in the collotype seems at first to end with a small curve to the right, of lighter shade. Neglecting this as perhaps not an ink mark, we have remaining a clear Ι with no sign of a continuation, that is to say, an *iota*. Before it is obviously ΤΟΥ, the article, as in lines 4, 12. The top of the Τ, which reaches nearly to the middle of the Υ, is not in line with the bar over Ι.Υ, of which the beginning from the Ι seems to have left faint traces and the end is clear. A small Ο, as in ΤΟΥ, would fit into Ι.Υ, making ΙΟΥ, a natural, though apparently quite exceptional abbreviation of 'Ιησοῦ, Jesus. Something is said below (p. 76) on the obvious objection that the kingdom 'of Jesus' would not have been spoken of in a saying introduced by 'Saith Jesus.'

2.

The Logia and Clem. R. II.

The *Ancient Homily* (p. 22) of pseudo-Clement is quoted below, with one slight alteration, from the translation in Bishop Lightfoot's *Apostolic Fathers*, Part I. vol. ii. 306–316 (1890):—

§ 1. 'Brethren, we ought so to think of Jesus Christ as of God ... we who were maimed in our understanding, and worshipped stocks and stones ... we recovered our sight, putting off by His will the cloud wherein we were wrapped.'

§§ 5-6. 'Wherefore, brethren, let us forsake our sojourn in this world and do the will of Him that called us, and let us not be afraid to depart out of this world ... ye know, brethren, that the sojourn of this flesh in this world is mean and for a short time, but the promise of Christ is great and marvellous, even the REST of the KINGDOM that shall be and of life eternal ... For, if we do the will of Christ, we shall find rest ... But ... with what confidence shall we, if we keep not our baptism pure and undefiled, enter into the kingdom of God?'

§ 9. 'Understand ye ... In what did ye recover your sight? if ye were not in this flesh ... If Christ the Lord who saved us, being first spirit, then became flesh, and so called us, in like manner also shall we in this flesh receive our reward ... While we have time to be healed, let us place ourselves in the hands of God the Physician.'

§ 12. 'Let us therefore await the kingdom of God betimes in love and righteousness, since we know not the day of God's appearing. For the Lord Himself, being asked by a certain person when His kingdom would come, said, *When the two shall be one, and the outside as the inside, and the male with the female, neither male nor female.*'

§ 14. '... for the scripture saith, *God made man male and female.* The male is Christ and the female is the Church ... for she was spiritual, as our Jesus also was spiritual, but was manifested in the last days that He might save us.'

§ 17. 'Herein He speaketh of the day of His appearing ... And the unbelievers ... shall be amazed when they see the KINGDOM of the world IN JESUS.'

The Logia are thought by some to be excerpts from the Gospel of the Egyptians, with which the Homilist was acquainted. He comes near to saying that the kingdom of God is the kingdom of Jesus, and may have known Logion II with the reading ΤΟΥ ΙΗϹΟΥ. In § 17 he writes, ἰδόντες τὸ βασίλειον τοῦ κόσμου ἐν τῷ Ἰησοῦ, when they see the kingdom of the world in Jesus (Rev. i. 9). 'There is ample authority for this sense of βασίλειον' (Lightfoot, p. 222).

In §§ 5-6 the rest (ἀνάπαυσις) of the kingdom to come and of life eternal is the reward of doing the will of Christ and renouncing the world. 'Ἀνάπαυσις is a LXX rendering of 'sabbath' or שבתון in Exod. xvi. 23, xxxi. 15, xxxv. 2; Lev. xvi. 31 (?), xxiii. 3, 24, 39, xxv. 4, 5, 8. The 'rest' of life eternal might have been suggested by verses of the New Testament, as Heb. iv. 9, Rev. xiv. 15; but the 'rest of the kingdom' corresponds remarkably with Logion II, in which finding the kingdom and sabbatizing are brought together. Others of the Logia are illustrated by words of the homilist. He uses the term 'fasting' only in its primary sense, but inculcates what he would have understood by fasting from the world. If he knew Logion V (B) as a saying of Jesus, he would not (we may infer) have read it in the pantheistic sense.

§ 12. *The male with the female.* 'This saying of the Egyptian Gospel, if it had any historical basis at all (which may be doubted), was perhaps founded on some utterance of our Lord similar in meaning to St. Paul's οὐκ ἔνι ἄρσεν καὶ θῆλυ, Gal. iii. 28 ... The name and idea of ἀρσενόθηλυς had their origin in the cosmical speculations embodied in heathen mythology' (Lightfoot, p. 239). The Midrash finds the idea of 'male-female' in the Bible.

Gen. i. 27, ii. 21-22, 24 (Matt. xix. 4-5): 'And God created man in his own image ... *male and female* created he them. And the Lord God ... took one of his ribs ... and the rib which the Lord God had taken from the man builded he into woman... Therefore shall a man leave his father and his mother, and shall cleave unto his wife: and they shall be one flesh.' In the Midrash (Gen. Rab. viii. 1, xvii. 6) it is said that God created the first man *androgynos*, cf. Plato, *Sympos.* 189 E, 191 D. Afterwards he took one of his two *sides* (Exod. xxvi. 26), and made it into woman. In Gen. ii. 24 the LXX inserts 'the two' thus, καὶ ἔσονται οἱ δύο εἰς σάρκα μίαν. This, with εἰς σάρκα omitted, may have become ἔσται τὰ δύο ἕν, whence as in the *Homily* ῞Οταν ἔσται τὰ δύο ἕν*.

Anastasius of Sinai speaks of ancient writers who

---

* The next clause in § 12 'is omitted in the quotation of Julius Cassianus' (Lightfoot, p. 238), perhaps rightly. There is a Talmudic phrase, 'one whose inside is as his outside' (*Jewish Fathers*, iii. n. 41).

applied the whole Hexaemeron *to Christ and the Church* (Lightfoot, p. 245). So St. Paul to the Ephesians (v. 31-32), with reference to Gen. ii. 24, 'I speak εἰς Χριστὸν καὶ [εἰς] τὴν ἐκκλησίαν.' According to the *Ancient Homily*, the kingdom of Jesus shall come when things shall be as they were in the beginning. 'Man without woman is not man' (*Jewish Fathers*, Addit. Note 4). He will be perfect (τέλειος) when the two are again one.

3.
The Logia and Barnabas.

At the end of Bishop Lightfoot's *St. Clement of Rome* (1890) there is an essay on the *Epistle of Barnabas*, in which the 'possible limits' of its date are said to be A.D. 70 and A.D. 132, and it is argued that we should 'place the so-called Barnabas during the reign of Vespasian (A.D. 70-79).' On the other hand, Keim, as quoted by Professor Sanday in *The Gospels in the Second Century*, is of opinion, that 'The Epistle of Barnabas ... was undoubtedly written at the time of the rebuilding of the temple under the Emperor Hadrian, about the year 120 A.D. ... at latest 130.'

The following passages of Barnabas are quoted from the edition by Dr. G. H. Rendall appended to Dr. W. Cunningham's *Dissertation on the Epistle of S. Barnabas* (1877):—

iii. 1-5. 'Therefore, touching these things, He saith again unto them, *To what purpose do ye make fasts unto me &c.*' Almost the whole chapter is a citation from Isaiah lviii.

vi. 12-19. '... as He saith to the Son, *Let us make man after our image and after our likeness, and let them rule over the beasts of the earth, and the fowls of the heaven, and the fish of the sea* ... He hath made *a second creation in these last days*: and the Lord saith, *Behold I make the last as the first* (τὰ ἔσχατα ὡς τὰ πρῶτα) ... And above we have said before, *And let them increase and multiply and rule over the fishes.* Who then is he that is able now to rule over beasts or fishes or fowls of the heaven ? ... So then though this cometh not to pass now, surely He hath told us when ... when we ourselves also are made perfect.' Did Barnabas know the Gospel of the Egyptians? There the Lord, in reply to the question 'When?,' makes *the last things as the first*, taking words from the Hexaemeron (p. 71) to symbolize man's ultimate return to his primal perfection.

vii. 3–11. 'In the writing of the commandment, *Whosoever keepeth* (lit. *fasteth*) *not the fast shall be utterly destroyed with death*, the Lord gave commandment, because He was in His own person about to offer the vessel of the Spirit as a sacrifice for our sins ... To this end ... "the goats like and equal," in order that when they behold Him coming in that day, they may be astonied at the likeness of the goat. See ye then in the goat the type of Jesus who should suffer ... Thus, He SAITH, *they who would see me, and lay hold of my kingdom, must through tribulation and suffering obtain me.*' These words of the Lord on the fast and His kingdom are not unlike a paraphrase of part of Logion II, on the remainder of which see under chap. xv. With 'astonied,' compare in the *Ancient Homily* (§ 17, p. 69), 'And the unbelievers shall be amazed.'

viii. 5–6. 'And why the wool upon wood? Because THE KINGDOM OF JESUS is upon the wood ... But wherefore the wool withal and the hyssop? Because in His kingdom there shall be days evil and polluted, in the which we shall be saved.'

xv. 1–7. 'Further, it hath been written concerning the Sabbath also in the Ten Words ... *And keep ye the Sabbath of the Lord holy with pure hands and a pure heart* ... *And He rested on the seventh day.* This signifieth, that when His Son shall come and utterly destroy this present time ... then He shall truly rest on the seventh day. Yea, and He saith furthermore, *Thou shalt keep it holy with pure hands and a pure heart.*' Current sayings of the type of Logion II (B) may be supposed to underlie the writer's addition to the Decalogue. Only the pure in heart can sabbatize the sabbath and see God.

4.

The Logia and Hermas.

Sim. i. 1-6. 'He saith to me, "Ye know that ye, who are the servants of God, are dwelling in a foreign land; for your city is far from this city... why do ye here prepare fields and expensive displays and buildings and dwelling-chambers which are superfluous?... as dwelling in a strange land prepare nothing more for thyself but a competency which is sufficient for thee...' (p. 439 sq., Harmer). The two cities are the world and the kingdom of God: the Christian is to be content with a bare sufficiency in the one, while he lays up for himself treasures in the other, i.e. he is to fast from the world that he may find the kingdom of God.

Sim. v. 1. Hermas is fasting, and the Shepherd comes to him and asks: 'What is this fast [that ye are fasting]?... Ye know not how to fast unto the Lord, neither is this a fast, this unprofitable fast which ye make unto Him,' οὐδέ ἐστιν νηστεία αὕτη ἡ ἀνωφελὴς ἣν νηστεύετε αὐτῷ (p. 347, Harmer), cf. *Epist. Barn.* § vii (p. 72), except ye fast the fast.' The Shepherd continues: 'But fast thou... such a fast as this; do no wickedness... let no evil desire rise up in thy heart...,' with the customary allusion for true fasting to Isaiah lviii (p. 17).

Sim. v. 2. 'Hear the parable which I shall tell thee relating to fasting.' A servant is ordered merely to fence a vineyard. He does more than is commanded; and the Master makes him joint-heir with 'his beloved Son, who was his heir.' In other words, as the reward of 'fasting the fast,' He gives him an inheritance in 'the kingdom of the Son of his love' (Col. i. 12-13).

Sim. v. 3. 'This then is the way that thou shalt keep this fast... First of all, keep thyself from every evil word and every evil desire, and purify thy heart from all the vanities of this WORLD' (αἰῶνος, as a synonym for κόσμου). Thus we have a paraphrase of 'fast from the world.'

Sim. ix. 7-9, 30-31. Of the round stones at first rejected by the builders, some remain round and useless, but others are squared and fitted into the tower; 'For this world and the vanities of their possessions must be cut off from them, and then they will fit into the kingdom of God.' The symbols used could not have expressed more exactly, 'Except ye fast from the world, ye shall not find place in the kingdom of God.'

The last clause of Logion V has been compared with the parable of the Willow, which represents (*Sim.* viii. 3) 'the law of God which was given to the whole world; and this law is the Son of God ...' (Huleatt). 'Cleave the tree, and there am I,' can scarcely rest upon the parable; but it may have been one of a number of sayings which the author had in mind when he wrote it. On 'Raise the stone' see p. 43.

5.

The Day of Atonement.

Logion II sums up sayings in passages of Leviticus and Isaiah read on the Day of Atonement or relating to it (p. 17). Barnabas finds in Lev. xvi on the two goats, which is a morning lesson for that day, types of Jesus and his coming kingdom. In the same section (p. 72) he quotes a verse of Leviticus with sayings of the Lord, who 'was in his own person about to offer the vessel of the Spirit as a sacrifice for our sins,' in the form :—

ὃς ἂν μὴ νηστεύσῃ τὴν νηστείαν θανάτῳ ἐξολοθρευθήσεται.

The verse belongs to the paragraph Lev. xxiii. 26-32:

'[26] And the Lord spake unto Moses, saying, [27] Also on the tenth of this seventh month is the day of atonement: it shall be a holy convocation unto you; and ye shall afflict your souls, and shall offer an offering made by fire unto the Lord. [28] And ye shall do no work in this same day: for it is a day of atonement, to make atonement for you before the Lord your God. [29] *For whatsoever soul shall not be afflicted in this same day shall be cut off from its people.* [30] And whatsoever soul shall do any work in this same day, I will destroy that soul from among its people. [31] No manner of

Conclusion

work shall ye do: it is a statute for ever to your generations in all your dwellings. ³²It is a sabbath of rest unto you, and ye shall afflict your souls: in the ninth of the month at even, from even unto even, shall ye celebrate (LXX σαββατιεῖτε) your sabbath.'

Barnabas may have quoted a current form of verse 29 with or without variation, but we have no reason to think that his words were all his own. In the Septuagint (Swete, i. 238) we read:

πᾶσα ψυχὴ ἥτις μὴ ταπεινωθήσεται ἐν αὐτῇ τῇ ἡμέρᾳ ταύτῃ ἐξολοθρευθήσεται ἐκ τοῦ λαοῦ αὐτῆς.

Field's *Hexapla* on the verse gives from 'another,' νηστεύσῃ ἐγκρατῶς, and in a footnote on a previous verse it quotes from Theodoret. *Quaest. ad Levit.*, ... νηστεῦσαι κελεύει ... ταπεινώσετε γάρ, φησί, τὰς ψυχὰς ὑμῶν. In a supposed saying of our Lord based upon the verse the 'people,' sc. of God, would quite naturally become the kingdom of God. Thus it is among the possibilities that there was a form of Logion II (A), 'Except ye *fast the fast* ye shall not find the kingdom of God (or Jesus).' From the same paragraph of Leviticus comes the phrase 'sabbatize the sabbath,' with reference to 'the fast' (Acts xxvii. 9). The true fast is a fast from worldly things, as Isaiah had said in effect (p. 18); and Hermas may have known the phrase, 'fast from the *cosmos*' (p. 73).

To what has been said on the sabbath as 'of the nature of a fast,' add from *Jewish Life in the Middle Ages* by Mr. Israel Abrahams (p. 172, 1896) that 'the fast' was of the nature of a feast:—

'There were no more joyous festivals in Israel than the fifteenth of Ab and the Day of Atonement. On these days the maidens of Jerusalem used to pass out in procession, arrayed in white garments, which all borrowed, in order not to put to the blush those who possessed no fitting attire of their own. They went out to the vineyards and danced. Then they sang—" Young man, lift up thine eyes and see whom thou art about to choose. Fix not thine eyes on beauty, but rather look to the piety of the bride's family.

Gracefulness is deceit, and beauty is a vain thing, but the woman who fears the Lord, she is worthy of praise."'
This is taken from the end of *Taanith* in the MISHNAH.

6.
Saith Jesus.

The obvious objection to Mr. Bartlet's reading in Logion II (p. 67) is that Jesus would not have spoken of the kingdom 'of Jesus.' But (1) ' Saith' sometimes introduces inexact citations, explanations, or paraphrases; and (2) words of others are said in a sense to be words of Jesus. The following instances seem to make it not incredible that the Logiographer should have prefixed his usual formula to a saying not purporting to be quoted exactly in the words of Jesus.

(1) On *Epist. Barn.* vii. 11, 'Thus, He saith, they who would see me and lay hold of my kingdom must through tribulation and suffering obtain me,' Dr. Rendall writes, 'This sentence is commonly quoted as one of the few apocryphal sayings of Christ ... I cannot consider the passage intended as such ... as a matter of fact φησίν is habitually used in this Epistle simply for *means, implies* ... more often so in fact than in introducing a direct quotation.' See also Resch, AGRAPHA *Logion* 10. Opinions may differ about the meaning of ' Saith' in particular cases, but λέγει and φησί are clearly sometimes explanatory.

In a note on '*This He saith*, keep the flesh pure and the seal unstained, to the end that we may receive life' (*Anc. Hom.* § 8), Bishop Lightfoot writes, ' τοῦτο λέγει] *He means this*: as in § 2 (twice), § 12. See the note on *Galatians* iii. 17.' A more or less close paraphrase with λέγει prefixed may be mistaken for a 'Logion,' and then quoted as such apart from its original context.

(2) *Epist. Barn.* v, 'For to this end the Lord endured to deliver His flesh unto corruption ... *For the scripture concerning Him containeth some things relating to Israel, and some things relating to us.* And it speaketh thus;

He was wounded for our transgressions ... We ought therefore to be very thankful unto the Lord, for that He both revealed unto us the past, and made us wise in the present, and as regards the future we are not without understanding. Now the scripture saith; *Not unjustly is the net spread for the birds.* He *meaneth* (λέγει) this, that a man shall justly perish, who having the knowledge of the way of righteousness forceth himself into the way of darkness ... Understand ye. *The prophets, receiving grace from Him, prophesied concerning Him'* (Harmer, p. 272 sq.).

Dr. Rendall's translation of v. 2 runs thus, 'For there are written concerning Him some things unto Israel, and some unto us. Now *Scripture* saith thus ...,' the Greek being γέγραπται γὰρ περὶ αὐτοῦ ἃ μὲν πρὸς τὸν Ἰσραήλ, ἃ δὲ πρὸς ἡμᾶς. λέγει δὲ οὕτως, *for there have been written concerning Him* ... *Now He* (or *it*) *saith thus.* The subject of 'saith' suggested by the context being 'He,' both editors bring in the 'Scripture' to avoid writing in effect, 'Jesus saith, Jesus was wounded for our transgressions.' But Barnabas regards Jesus as prophesying in the prophets. 'What then saith He in the prophet? *And let them eat of the goat that is offered at the fast for all their sins.* Attend carefully; *And let all the priests alone eat the entrails unwashed with vinegar.* Wherefore? Since ye are to give Me, who am to offer my flesh for the sins of My new people, gall with vinegar to drink, eat ye alone, while the people fasteth and waileth in sackcloth and ashes; that He might shew that He must suffer at their hands' (vii. 4–5, Harmer).

7.

The Language of the Logia.

Writers on the Logia have raised the question whether their original language was Semitic, and it has been discussed in a suggestive way by Professor Cersoy of Lyon in *Quelques Remarques sur les Logia de Behnesa* published in the *Revue Biblique* of July, 1898.

LOGION II. ἐὰν μὴ νηστεύσητε τὸν κόσμον. 'The words "fast the world" have no sense except we think of the rabbinical expression נזיר עולם, a Nazarite of the world, which means a life-long ascetic' (Kohler). When νηστεύειν is followed by an accusative in Biblical Greek, it is either that of the cognate noun (νηστεύειν νηστείαν), or that of duration (νηστεύειν ... ἡμέρας). 'It would seem,' it has been said, 'that if τὸν κόσμον is to stand here, it must be taken in the latter sense. In this connexion we should have expected (εἰς) τὸν αἰῶνα (1 Cor. viii. 13); but there may have been reasons why τὸν κόσμον was preferred in the present context.'

Professor Cersoy postulates a Semitic original of the Logion, meaning 'Si vous ne jeûnez pas le jeûne ...', in which a translator mistook צום (Heb.) or צומא (Aram.), *fast*, for עלם or עלמא, *world*.

Barnabas, however, has the construction (§ vii. p. 72) 'fast the fast' in his version of Lev. xxiii. 29, 'whatsoever soul shall not *be afflicted*' (Heb., Onk., Syr.). Targ. Jerus. reads, '... for every son of man that can fast (לציימא) and does not fast in that self-same day shall be destroyed by death from among his people.' Thus a Semitic original of 'fast the fast' would not necessarily have had צום or צומא, *fast* ; and the construction νηστεύειν νηστείαν may have been introduced by a translator, like 'die the death' in the Latin of *Epist. Barn.* loc. cit., 'ut si quis non ieiunaret ieiunium, morte moreretur.'

On the first publication of the Logia I defended νηστεύειν τὸν κόσμον as possibly a construction in actual use (p. 10, § 1). This view has been taken by others, cf. from a recent private letter, 'The accusative after νηστεύειν is not unlike that after πεινῆν and διψῆν in late and New Testament Greek' (I. B.). If there was one form of the Logion with 'fast *the fast*,' this might have led to the use of the accusative in another form of it with 'fast *the world*.'

In Logion II (B) 'sabbatize the sabbath' is no doubt from a rendering of a Hebrew phrase, but it does not follow that the whole Logion must have been originally

Conclusion

in Hebrew. On the other hand it may be said in favour of a Semitic original, that Lev. xxiii. 32, to which we suppose the Logion refer, runs thus in Targ. Jerus.:

. . ., תְּהֵוַן צָיְימִין צוֹמְכוֹן (צוֹמֵיכוֹן or) וְשַׁבְּתִין שׁוּבְּתֵיכוֹן . . .,

Ye shall be fasting your fast (or *fasts*) *and sabbathing your sabbaths and keeping the times of your assemblies with* GLADNESS (p. 75). See in the Pentateuch with three Targums, ed. S. Netter, Lev. 76 *a* (Wien, 1859). For the construction 'fast a fast' in Hebrew compare Zech. vii. 5 הֲצוֹם צַמְתֻּנִי אָנִי.

LOGION V. *Why raise the stone, but cleave the tree?* Professor Cersoy makes the ingenious suggestion that some translator, sc. from a Hebrew original, read הצב with *hé* (*hiph.* from נצב) '*dresse*, ou *érige*,' by mistake for חצב with *cheth*, '*taille*, ou *creuse*.' But the saying is variously interpreted; and on a certain view of it the contrast, 'raise,' 'cleave,' may have been intended to be significant, see in Exod. xx. 25 *not . . . of hewn stone* (p. 35), and compare the symbolism of unhewn stones in Hermas, Irenaeus, and other patristic writers.

LOGION VI. *Neither doth a physician do cures to them that know him.* Professor Cersoy, putting together passages from the Peshitto, concludes : ' Par conséquent, la locution araméenne citée répond exactement au grec θεραπείας ποιέω.' It is also pointed out that 'them that know him' is a Hebraism (p. 57), and the question is asked, Why did the redactor not write εἰς τοὺς γνωστοὺς αὐτοῦ ? But it may be remarked that the phrase used is exactly what was wanted : the case supposed is that of a physician who fails to cure ' them that know him' because they know him, not from any fault or weakness or prejudice on his part arising from the fact that he knows them.

8.

Sources of the Logia.

What remains of Logion I may be an extract from one of the Synoptic Gospels, and others of the Logia may be developments from one or more of the Four Gospels; or the Logia may all be extracts from some other writing or writings, which agreed more or less nearly in places with the Canonical Gospels.

Messrs. Grenfell and Hunt (G. H. p. 16) considered 'the possibility, which the *provenance* of the papyrus naturally suggests, that our fragment may come from the *Gospel according to the Egyptians.*' This view was shortly afterwards advocated by Mr. F. P. Badham in the *Athenæum* (Aug. 7, 1897), and it is adopted by Professor Harnack.

Mr. Badham in the *Athenæum* of Dec. 31, 1898, begins by quoting three passages bearing on the Egyptian Gospel:—

(1) 'No one who does not fast all his days shall see God. ... No one who is not a virgin all his days is able to see God. ... No one who does not leave father and mother and brother and sister and children and houses and all that he hath, and go out after our Lord, is able to see God.—W. Wright's *Syriac Apocrypha: Transitus Mariae* (sic), pp. 43-46.'

(2) 'The internal I have made external and the external internal.—Wright's *Apocryphal Acts,* vol. ii, *Acta Thomae,* p. 282.'

(3) 'We [Guardian Angels] have come from holy men who have renounced the world ... some of them dwell in caves, others in holes of the earth ... thirsty for thy name's sake ... And the voice of God answered them, Know ye, my angels, that ye are here, but my grace and my remembrance, which is my Son, is with them.—*Apocalypsis Pauli*, ed. Tischendorf, pp. 38, 39.'

It is added, '... there seems a strong probability that the Egyptian Evangelist utilized the post-Resurrection standpoint ... But the *Acta Thomae,* which have so strangely escaped notice, entail much more important consequences, especially in their Syriac form ... "And when he hath found rest he becometh a king" (Wright, p. 270) recalls 2 Clement v ... Such expressions as "Blessed are the bodies of the pure, worthy to become clean temples in which the Messiah shall dwell," recall Hermas and the *Acta Theclae,* whose affinities with one another, and with 2 Clement, have already given

Conclusion

rise to suspicions of Egyptian indebtedness (see Resch's *Agrapha*, pp. 433-5), and, it may incidentally be added, strengthen the connexion of Hermas (*Sim.* v. 3), "Thus then shall you observe the fast... Purify your heart from all the vanities of this world," with Logion 2.'

'The early references to anchorites in Barnabas iv. and Eusebius *H. E.* vi. 9, 10, allow one, as I pointed out in the *Athenæum* (August 7, 1897), to understand Logion 4 [=v] as a recommendation to seek Christ in the stocks and stones of the desert.'

On the Gospel according to the Egyptians see Harnack on the Logia* (p. 27 sq., 1897), and in his *Chron. der altchr. Litteratur*, comparing Clem. R. II, ed. Lightfoot. Its resemblance in places to the Synoptic Gospels is, so far as it goes, consistent with the theory that it contained all the Oxyrhynchus Logia. On the other hand it is possible that they were severally extracted or evolved from the canonical and other writings.

The Old Testament.—From whatever sources the Logiographer drew his materials, some things in the Logia may be traced back to, or may have been suggested by, the Old Testament. With Logion III compare in the Book of Proverbs (i-viii) the sayings of Wisdom, who 'stands' on the 'habitable earth,' and admonishes the 'sons of men.'

9.

The Compilation.

The small fragment containing the Logia 'measures $5\frac{3}{4} \times 3\frac{3}{4}$ inches, but its height was originally somewhat greater' (G. H. p. 6). So far as it goes, the evidence supports the view that we have before us 'a leaf from an ancient *cheap and portable* copy' of sayings attributed to our Lord (Abbott, p. 2). The Logia 'are probably from

---

* Professor Harnack's tract on the Logia has also been published in English in vol. vi of the fifth series of the *Expositor* (1897).

the *Vade Mecum*' of a Christian of the middle of the second century (Huleatt).

Intent upon giving *multum in parvo*, the Logiographer has detached sayings of the Lord from their settings in some form of the Gospel narrative, and introduced them abruptly in his booklet with the words, 'Saith Jesus.' Thus Logion V, as Professor Harnack remarks (*Expositor*, p. 403), is clearly 'taken from a larger context; for we have to supply the fact that the Lord is here speaking of His disciples.' 'In the other cases also there is no indication of the occasion; this cannot be primary; the compiler was concerned only with the Saying, and he left out the occasion.'

Thinking of spiritual applications, he can compress two or more sayings into one without regard to verbal congruity or logical sequence. Logion VII, for example (pp. 58–62), confuses two sayings which have been preserved separately in the Gospels as they have come down to us. Clearly (1) this Logion is not a survival from an independent and primitive tradition. But (2) the redactor's free handling of canonical sayings and his correlation with them of so much that is not canonical point to a more or less early date, at which the fringe of Apocrypha had not yet been cut away from the New Testament Scriptures.

APOCRYPHAL GOSPELS

THE APOCRYPHAL GOSPELS

I

Among the *Cambridge Essays* of the year 1856 is an instructive and interesting dissertation on APOCRYPHAL GOSPELS by C. J. Ellicott, M.A., late Fellow of St. John's College, now Bishop of Gloucester, which is in part a review of Tischendorf's *Evangelia Apocrypha* (Lips. 1853). In the following pages on the Oxyrhynchus Logia and some Apocryphal Gospels the volume *Evangelia Apocrypha* is quoted from the edition of 1876. We begin with a translation of *Evangelium Thomae Graece* from the latter and shorter of Tischendorf's two recensions of it.

EVANGELIUM THOMAE B (Tisch. p. 158 sq.).

Book of the holy Apostle Thomas concerning the conversation (ἀναστροφῆς) in childhood of the Lord.

CHAPTER I.

I, Thomas the Israelite, thought it needful to acquaint all the brethren that are of the Gentiles with the mighty works of His childhood which our Lord Jesus Christ did while He had His conversation bodily in the city of Nazareth, when He had come to the fifth year of His age.

CHAPTER II.

One day, when it had rained, He went out of the house where His mother was, and was playing on the ground where waters were flowing down. And when He had made pools, the waters were coming down, and the pools were filled with water. Then saith He, I will that ye become clear and good waters. And straightway they became so. But a certain child of Annas the scribe passing by, and carrying a stick of willow, upset the pools with the stick, and the waters were poured out. And Jesus turned and said to him, Wicked and lawless one, what harm did the pools do thee that thou didst empty them? Thou shalt not go thy way, and thou shalt dry up like the stick which thou holdest. And as he was going, after a little, he fell down and gave up the ghost. And when the young children that were playing with Him saw, they marvelled and went and told the father of him that was dead. And he ran and found the young child dead, and went and complained to Joseph.

Chapter III.

And Jesus made of that clay twelve sparrows: and it was Sabbath. And one young child ran and told Joseph, saying, Behold, thy young child playeth about the runnel, and hath made sparrows of the clay, which is not lawful. And he when he heard went, and saith to the young child, Why doest thou these things, profaning the Sabbath? And Jesus answered him not, but looked at the sparrows, and saith, Go, fly, and remember me while ye live. And at the word they flew and went off into the air. And Joseph when he saw marvelled.

Chapter IV.

And after some days, as Jesus was passing by through the midst of the city, a certain young child threw a stone at Him, and hit Him on the shoulder. And Jesus said to him, Thou shalt not go thy way. And straightway he too fell down and died. And they that chanced to be there were astonished, saying, Whence is this young child, that every word that He saith hath immediate effect? But they too went and complained against Joseph, saying, Thou wilt not be able to dwell with us in this city. But if thou please, teach thy young child to bless and not to curse; for He slayeth our young children, and every word that He saith hath immediate effect.

Chapter V.

And when Joseph was seated upon his chair, the young child stood before him. And he took hold of Him by the ear, and pinched it hard. And Jesus looked intently at him and said, It is enough for thee.

Chapter VI.

And on the morrow he took Him by the hand, and led Him to a certain rabbi (καθηγητής) named Zacchaeus, and saith to him, Take this young child, rabbi, and teach him letters. And he saith, Deliver Him to me, brother, and I will teach Him the Scripture, and persuade Him to bless all, and not curse. And when Jesus heard, He laughed, and saith unto them, Ye say what things ye know, but I understand more things than ye; for before the ages I am. And I know when your fathers' fathers were born, and I understand how many are the years of your life. And one that heard was astonished. And again Jesus said to them, Marvel ye that I said unto you, that I know how many are the years of your life? Of a truth I know when the world was created. Behold, ye believe me not now. When ye see my cross, then will ye believe that I say things true. And they were astonished when they heard these things.

Chapter VII.

And Zacchaeus wrote the alphabet in Hebrew, and saith unto Him, Alpha. And the young child saith, Alpha. And again the teacher, Alpha, and the young child likewise. Then again the teacher a third time, the Alpha. Then Jesus looking at the rabbi saith, Thou that knowest not the Alpha, how shalt thou teach another the Beta? And the young child, beginning from the Alpha, said of Himself the twenty-two letters. Then, moreover, again He saith, Hear, teacher, the array of the first letter, and know how many strokes and rules it hath, and joint marks diametral and convergent. And when Zacchaeus heard such attributes of the one letter, he was astonished, and could not answer Him. And he turned and said to Joseph, Brother, of a truth this young child is not earth-born: take Him then away from me.

Chapter VIII.

And after these things, one day Jesus was playing with other children on a house-top. And one young child was pushed down by another and thrown headlong upon the ground and died. And when the children playing with him saw it they fled; and Jesus was left alone standing upon the housetop, where the boy was thrown headlong. And when the parents of the dead child learned it, they ran with weeping, and when they found the child down on the ground lying dead, and Jesus standing up above, supposing that it was by Him that the boy had been thrown headlong, they looked intently at Him, and reproached Him. And Jesus, when He saw, straightway leaped down from the house-top, and stood at the head of him that was dead, and saith to him, Zeno, did I cast thee down? arise and speak—for so was the boy called. And at the word the boy arose, and he worshipped Jesus and said, Lord, Thou didst not cast me down, but when I was dead Thou broughtest me to life.

Chapter IX.

And after a few days, a certain one of the neighbours in cleaving a tree cut off the base of his foot with the axe, and from loss of blood was at the point of death. And much people running together, Jesus also came with them there. And He touched the wounded foot of the young man, and straightway healed him; and He saith to him,

Arise, cleave thy wood. And he arose and worshipped Him, giving thanks and cleaving the wood. Likewise, also, all that were there marvelled and gave Him thanks.

CHAPTER X.

And when He was six years old, Mary, His mother, sent Him to fetch water from the well. And as He went His pitcher was broken. And going on to the well, He spread out His upper garment, and drew water from the well, and filled it, and took and brought away the water to His mother. And she, when she saw, was astonished and embraced and kissed Him.

CHAPTER XI.

And when He had reached the eighth year of His age, Joseph was ordered by a certain rich man to construct a bedstead for him, for he was a carpenter. And he went out in the field to collect wood, and Jesus also went with him. And having cut two pieces of wood, and lopped the one, he laid it beside the other; and when he had measured he found it too stunted. And when he saw he was grieved, and sought to find another. And when Jesus saw He saith to him, Lay these two together, so as to make both ends level. And Joseph being in doubt what the young child meant by this, did what was ordered. And He saith to him again, Take firm hold of the stunted piece of wood. And Joseph marvelling took hold of it. Then also Jesus taking hold of the further extremity pulled at its other end, and made that piece of wood equal to the other. And He saith to Joseph, Grieve no more, but do thy work without hindrance. And he, when he saw, marvelled beyond measure, and saith within himself, Blessed am I that God gave me such a child. And when they had gone away into the city, Joseph told Mary. And she when she heard and saw the strange mighty works of her Son rejoiced, glorifying Him with the Father and the Holy Ghost, now and ever and unto the ages of the ages. Amen.

II

PARALLELS TO LOGIA.

1.

In Logion III (B) Jesus says of the sons of men * that they are *blind in their heart* (cf. Mark iii. 5 Vulg.), the last complete line on the *verso* of the papyrus being,

ΟΤΙ ΤΥΦΛΟΙ ΕΙCΙΝ ΤΗ ΚΑΡ,

which would make the reading as far as καρδίᾳ certain, even if nothing more remained. But there are faint traces of letters below on the ragged edge of the page, from which it has been conjectured (p. 29) that the Logion probably continued thus,

ΔΙΑ ΑΥΤΩΝ ΚΑΙ ΟΥ ΒΛΕ
ΠΟΥCΙΝ.

The expression 'blind in heart' can be illustrated by figures of speech akin to it, but the exact phrase seems to be of rare occurrence. It occurs again in the Gospel of Thomas, where in chapter viii of the longer Greek recension we read (Tisch. p. 148):—

Τῶν δὲ Ἰουδαίων παραινούντων τῷ Ζακχαίῳ, ἐγέλασε τὸ παιδίον μέγα καὶ εἶπεν· Νῦν καρποφορείτωσαν τὰ σά, καὶ βλεπέτωσαν οἱ τυφλοὶ τῇ καρδίᾳ.

And as the Jews were encouraging Zacchaeus, the young child laughed greatly and said, Now let thine occupations be fruitful, and *let the blind in heart see.*

Nothing like this is to be found in the short Greek recension or in the Latin. In the Syriac 'blind' takes the place of 'blind in heart,' and so in *pseudo-Matthew*, chap. xxxi, thus (Tisch. p. 102):—

'Tunc Iesus laeto vultu subridens de eo dixit cum imperio cunctis filiis Israel astantibus et audientibus:

---

* Cf. Psalm iv. 3, υἱοὶ ἀνθρώπων, ἕως πότε βαρυκάρδιοι;

Parallels to Logia 91

Fructificent infructuosi et *videant caeci* et claudi ambulent recte et *pauperes* fruantur bonis et reviviscant mortui.'

Thus the phrase 'blind in heart,' which has so narrowly escaped obliteration from the Oxyrhynchus papyrus, has been lost or reduced to the one word 'blind' in the Apocryphal Gospels, except in the short Greek recension of *Evang. Thomae*. The saying of Jesus in this Gospel,

$$\beta\lambda\epsilon\pi\acute{\epsilon}\tau\omega\sigma\alpha\nu\ o\acute{\iota}\ \tau\upsilon\phi\lambda o\grave{\iota}\ \tau\hat{\eta}\ \kappa\alpha\rho\delta\acute{\iota}\alpha,$$

corresponds remarkably with His words in the Logion as conjecturally restored,

$$\tau\upsilon\phi\lambda o\grave{\iota}\ \tau\hat{\eta}\ \kappa\alpha\rho\delta\acute{\iota}\alpha\ \kappa\alpha\grave{\iota}\ o\mathring{\upsilon}\ \beta\lambda\acute{\epsilon}\pi o\upsilon\sigma\iota\nu.$$

Having regard to the way in which the Apocryphal Gospels were made up, we may think it quite possible that a traditional saying of our Lord about the *blind in heart* who *see not* underlies the saying of the 'young child' happily preserved in one of them, *Let the blind in heart see.*

2.

Restoring the phrase 'blind in heart' in the Latin parallel to *Evang. Thomae*, B. viii, we should have in *pseudo-Matt.* xxxi, as cited above, *caeci corde*, followed by *pauperes*. This further confirms the conjecture that Logion IV on 'poverty' should be read as a continuation of Logion III (B) on the 'blind in heart.'

3.

'It is indeed strange that there should be no signs in literature of the remarkable saying, "Raise the stone, &c." But we must remember that several Agrapha, hardly less remarkable, rest upon a single quotation (e. g. ὁ θαυμάσας βασιλεύσει κ. τ. λ.). If that one quotation had been wanting, the saying would have been lost sight of altogether' (L. S. p. 43). Perhaps, however, Logion V is referred to in the Gospel of Thomas.

With *Evang. Thomae*, B. ix (p. 88 sq.) compare A. x: 'After a few days, as a certain young man was cleaving wood in the *neighbourhood*, the axe fell and cut through the base of his foot, and from loss of blood he was at the point of death. And when there was a clamour and a running together, the young child Jesus also ran there. And He forced His way through the crowd, and took hold of the young man's wounded foot, and straightway it was healed. And He said to the young man, Arise now : cleave the wood, and remember me. And the crowd seeing what had come to pass worshipped the young child, saying, Of a truth the Spirit of God dwelleth in this young child.'

The Greek texts of this story in the two recensions are as follows :—

A. Cap. x (Tisch. p. 150 sq.): Μετ' ὀλίγας ἡμέρας σχίζων τις ξύλα ἐν τῇ γωνίᾳ νεώτερος, ἔπεσεν ἡ ἀξίνη καὶ διέσχισεν τὴν βάσιν τοῦ ποδὸς αὐτοῦ, καὶ ἔξαιμος γενόμενος ἀπέθνησκεν. Θορύβου δὲ γενομένου καὶ συνδρομῆς, ἔδραμε καὶ τὸ παιδίον Ἰησοῦς ἐκεῖ. καὶ βιασάμενος διῆλθεν τὸν ὄχλον, καὶ ἐκράτησεν τοῦ νεανίσκου τὸν πεπληγότα πόδαν, καὶ εὐθέως ἰάθη. εἶπε δὲ τῷ νεανίσκῳ· ἀνάστα νῦν. σχίζε τὰ ξύλα καὶ μνημόνευέ μου. ὁ δὲ ὄχλος ἰδὼν τὸ γεγονὸς προσεκύνησαν τὸ παιδίον, λέγοντες· ἀληθῶς πνεῦμα θεοῦ ἐνοικεῖ ἐν τῷ παιδίῳ τούτῳ.

B. Cap. ix (Tisch. p. 161 sq.): Καὶ μετ' ὀλίγας ἡμέρας σχίζων τις τῶν γειτόνων ξύλον ἀπέτεμε τὴν βάσιν τοῦ ποδὸς αὐτοῦ διὰ τοῦ πελέκυος, καὶ ἔξαιμος γεγονὼς ἤμελλεν ἀποθνήσκειν. Καὶ λαοῦ συνδεδραμηκότος πολλοῦ συνῆλθεν καὶ ὁ Ἰησοῦς ἐκεῖ. καὶ ἁψάμενος τοῦ πεπληγμένου ποδὸς τοῦ νεανίσκου, καὶ εὐθέως ἰάσατο αὐτόν. καί φησιν αὐτῷ· ἀνάστα, σχίσον τὰ ξύλα σου. καὶ ἀναστὰς προσεκύνησεν αὐτόν, εὐχαριστῶν καὶ σχίζων τὰ ξύλα. ὁμοίως καὶ πάντες οἱ ὄντες ἐκεῖ θαυμάσαντες ηὐχαρίστησαν αὐτῷ.

Tischendorf in *Evangelia Apocrypha* sometimes corrects clerical errors, and sometimes merely calls attention to them. On πόδαν in *Evang. Thomae*, A. x, he writes, 'ita uterque codex.' At the beginning of the same chapter he writes γωνίᾳ, where 'uterque codex γονίᾳ.' But in the translation given above the true reading is assumed to be ἐν τῇ γειτονίᾳ, a phrase found at the beginning of A. xvii (Tisch. p. 155), 'And after these things, *in the neighbourhood* of Joseph, a certain infant fell ill and died.'

The story told in *Evang. Thomae*, A. x and B. ix may

have been founded partly upon the latter clause of Logion V (B),

Ἔγειρον τὸν λίθον κἀκεῖ εὑρήσεις με.
Σχίσον τὸ ξύλον κἀγὼ ἐκεῖ εἰμί.

ἐκεῖ] A salient word in the Logion is ΕΚΕΙ, *there*. It is preserved in the Greek recensions of *Evang. Thomae*, according to both of which there is one alone cleaving wood, and Jesus runs and comes with the crowd *there*.

The significance of the word having been forgotten, it was passed over in the Latin (Tisch. p. 174):—

'Post paucos vero dies puer quidam in ipso vico findebat ligna percussitque pedem suum. Et cum venisset turba multa ad eum, *venit et Iesus cum illis*. Et tetigit pedem qui laesus fuerat, et subito sanus factus est. Dixit autem ei Iesus : Surge et finde ligna et memora mei. Cum autem vidisset turba signa quae cum eo facta sunt, adoraverunt Iesum et dixerunt: Vere certissime credimus quia deus est.'

In another form of the narrative (Tisch., p. 174 n.) we read, 'Et cum turba vicinorum cucurrisset ad eum, *venit Iesus*, unxit in pede illius &c.,' where again there is no word for ἐκεῖ.

σχίσον τὸ ξύλον] In *Evang. Thomae*, A. x and B. ix respectively, we have in the narrative σχίζων ξύλα and σχίζων ξύλον, and in the saying of Jesus σχίζε τὰ ξύλα and σχίσον τὰ ξύλα σου, while in both recensions, as we have seen, we find ἐκεῖ, which occurs twice in the Logion.

The Logion having perhaps suggested the saying of Jesus to the woodcutter, details of the narrative not accounted for by the Logion may either have been drawn from other sources, or simply invented by the pseudo-Evangelist.

Twenty years ago, Dr. J. M. Cotterill in his *Peregrinus Proteus* pointed out that some curious things in the Gospel of Thomas may have been suggested by verses of the Old Testament.

The story of the broken pitcher (p. 89) runs thus in A. xi: 'And when He was six years old, His mother sent Him to draw water and bring it to the house, having given

Him a pitcher. And He being jostled in the crowd, the pitcher was broken. But Jesus spread out the cloak which He wore, and filled it with water, and brought it to His mother. And when His mother saw the miracle which was done, she kissed Him, and kept in herself the mysteries which she saw Him do.'

Compare *pseudo-Matthew*, xxxiii (Tisch. p. 103):—

'Erat autem Iesus annorum sex, et misit illum mater sua cum hydria ad fontem haurire aquam cum infantibus. Et contigit postquam hausit aquam, ut quidam ex infantibus impegerit eum et conquassaverit hydriam et fregerit eam. At Iesus expandit pallium quo utebatur, et suscepit in pallio suo tantum aquae quantum erat in hydria, et portavit eam matri suae. At illa videns mirabatur, et cogitabat intra se, et condebat omnia haec in corde suo.'

According to another account, a girl is sent for the water, and her pitcher is broken at the well. Then Jesus comes, carries water in His cloak to His mother, and also by His word joins the fragments of the pitcher together (Tisch. p. 103 n.):—

'Cum beata Maria misisset puellam suam cum hydria, et multitudo mulierum ad fontem coadunata fuisset, propter pressuram eorum fracta est hydria quam dominica puella portaverat. Tunc pervenit Iesus ad fontem, implevit pallium suum aqua et tulit matri suae. Deinde colligens fragmenta hydriae insimul iungens verbo suo solidavit ita quod scissurae in ea signum minime videretur. Tunc beata Maria osculata est Iesum dicens: Benedictus sit Deus qui nobis talem filium dedit.' There is a reading, 'Et cum venisset ad *puteum*,' cf. in *Ev. Thom. Lat.* ix, 'Cumque venisset Iesus ad fontem vel ad *puteum*' (Tisch. p. 174 sq.).

Comparing *Evang. Thomae*, B. x, ἐκ τῆς πηγῆς ... συνετρίβη ἡ ὑδρία κ. τ. λ., and the other versions of the story, we may conclude that it is based partly on Eccles. xii. 6, 'and the pitcher is broken at the well,' LXX καὶ συντριβῇ ἡ ὑδρία ἐπὶ τὴν πηγήν. The words *pitcher* and *well* in the translation on p. 89 will serve to remind the reader of Ecclesiastes in the Authorized Version.

Parallels to Logia

The use of one of His garments by Jesus in place of a waterpot was probably suggested by Prov. xxx. 4:
Who hath gathered the wind in his fists?
Who hath bound the waters in his garment?
Who hath established all the ends of the earth?
What is his name, and what is his son's name, if thou knowest?

Dr. Cotterill, before the finding of the Logia, suggested that the story of the woodcutter in the Gospel of Thomas is founded upon the verse Eccles. x. 9, which some suppose to be referred to in Logion V, 'Whoso removeth stones shall be hurt therewith; and *he that cleaveth wood* (σχίζων ξύλα) *shall be endangered thereby.*' Gregory Thaumaturgus, it was added, wrote in his *Metaphrasis* of Ecclesiastes, that a woodcutter is in danger from his own axe, the head of which may fall from the handle, ἀλλὰ καὶ σχίζων ξύλα ἐν αὐτῷ τῷ οἰκείῳ ὅπλῳ τὸν κίνδυνον οἴσει· ἐὰν δὲ ξυμβῇ τοῦ στελεοῦ τὸν πέλεκυν ἐκπηδῆσαι, θορυβηθήσεται ὁ ταῦτα ἐργαζόμενος. 'In Eccles. there is no mention of an axe. In *Evang. Thom.* B, πέλεκυς is the word; in A, ἀξίνη; and in the latter θορύβου γενομένου is said. The words σχίζων ξύλα are in both versions.'

The author of the story in *Evang. Thomae* may have used the *Metaphrasis*; or Gregory may be thought to have used *Evang. Thomae*, which in some form existed at an early date; or, writing independently of one another, they may both have used 2 Kings vi. 5, 'But as one was felling a beam, the axe head fell into the water.' This with Eccles. x. 9 and without the *Metaphrasis* may have suggested the accident to the woodcutter in *Evang. Thomae*. Logion V would then account for the appearance of Jesus ἐκεῖ, *there*, and for His words, *Cleave τὰ ξύλα*, or *Cleave τὰ ξύλα σου*, the word for *Cleave* being in *Evang. Thomae* B, σχίσον, exactly as in the Logion.

4.

If Logion V and Eccles. x. 9 were used in the story of the woodcutter, it may be thought that somewhere in the

Apocryphal Gospels there should be, or have been, a reference to the *stone* or stones of the Logion and Ecclesiastes. In *Evang. Thomae*, B. iv (p. 86) there is a story about a stone, but in the parallel passages of *Evangelia Apocrypha* the 'stone' has fallen out. Thus in *Evang. Thomae*, A. iv, we read (Tisch. p. 143):—

Εἶτα πάλιν ἐπορεύετο διὰ τῆς κώμης, καὶ παιδίον τρέχων διερράγη εἰς τὸν ὦμον αὐτοῦ,

and in cap. v of the Latin (ib. p. 168):—

'Et post paucos dies deambulante Iesu cum Ioseph per villam concurrit de infantibus unus et percussit Iesum in ulnas,' without mention of the stone in either version.

The Greek of B. iv on the stone is as follows (Tisch. p. 159):—

Μετὰ δέ τινας ἡμέρας διερχομένου τοῦ Ἰησοῦ μέσον τῆς πόλεως, παιδίον τι ῥίψαν λίθον κατ' αὐτοῦ ἔπληξεν αὐτοῦ τὸν ὦμον. καὶ εἶπεν αὐτῷ ὁ Ἰησοῦς· Οὐκ ἀπελεύσει τὴν ὁδόν σου. καὶ εὐθέως καταπεσὼν κἀκεῖνος ἀπέθανεν. οἱ δὲ τυχόντες ἐξεπλάγησαν λέγοντες· πόθεν τὸ παιδίον τοῦτό ἐστιν, ὅπως πᾶν ῥῆμα ὃ λέγει ἔργον γίνεται ἔτοιμον; Ἀλλὰ κἀκεῖνοι ἀπελθόντες ἐγκάλουν (*sic*) πρὸς Ἰωσὴφ λέγοντες κ.τ.λ.

This is a more likely account of the matter. The child having maliciously thrown a stone at Jesus, his mischief recoils upon himself and occasions his death (p. 86), in accordance with Prov. xxvi. 27:

Whoso diggeth a pit shall fall therein:
And he that rolleth a stone, it shall return upon him.

This verse alone might have suggested to pseudo-Thomas the child's throwing of a stone with fatal consequence to the thrower; but it does not account for the part which Jesus plays in the story, which, like the story of the woodcutter, may have been made up from two or more sources in combination. We have to consider whether it refers to Logion V and Eccles. x. 8-9:

He that diggeth a pit shall fall into it;
And whoso breaketh an hedge, a serpent shall bite him.
Whoso removeth stones shall be hurt therewith;
He that cleaveth wood shall be endangered thereby.

Parallels to Logia

Whoso removeth &c.] In Field's *Hexapla*, Symmachus is quoted for the rendering μετεωρῶν λίθους κακωθήσεται, *one raising stones into mid-air shall be injured*. If the clause could be so rendered, it could be made to mean the same as 'he that rolleth a stone &c.' in the verse Prov. xxvi. 27, the first hemistich of which agrees with Eccles. x. 8 *a*.

A like turn might then have been given to ἔγειρον τὸν λίθον, the words following which in the Logion may have suggested the presence of Jesus ἐκεῖ, *there*.

A serpent shall bite him] Supposing the pseudo-Thomas to have had this in mind incidentally as part of a passage of Scripture which he had been using as suggested, the reader may think that he ought to have made up a story about the 'serpent.' Accordingly we read in *Evang. Thomae*, A. xvi (Tisch. p. 154 sq.):—

Ἔπεμψε δὲ Ἰωσὴφ τὸν υἱὸν αὐτοῦ τὸν Ἰάκωβον τοῦ δῆσαι ξύλα καὶ φέρειν εἰς τὸν οἶκον αὐτοῦ· ἠκολούθει δὲ καὶ τὸ παιδίον Ἰησοῦς αὐτῷ. καὶ συλλέγοντος τοῦ Ἰακώβου τὰ φρύγανα, ἔχιδνα ἔδακε τὴν χεῖραν Ἰακώβου. Καὶ κατατειναμένου αὐτοῦ καὶ ἀπολλυμένου προσήγγισεν ὁ Ἰησοῦς καὶ κατεφύσησε τὸ δῆγμα· καὶ εὐθέως ἐπαύσατο ὁ πόνος, καὶ τὸ θηρίον ἐρράγη, καὶ πάραυτα ἔμεινεν * ὁ Ἰάκωβος ὑγιής.

Joseph sends his son James to gather wood. As he is gathering the *sticks*, a *viper* bites *his hand*. Jesus who is there blows upon the bite: the pain ceases: the *beast* bursts: and James remains whole. Jesus—not according to the Logion—healing one of 'them that knew Him.'

This refers obviously to Acts xxviii. 3–5:

'But when Paul had gathered a bundle of *sticks*, and laid them on the fire, there came a *viper* out of the heat, and fastened on *his hand*. . . . And he shook off the *beast* into the fire, and felt no harm.'

Nevertheless, the story in *Evang. Thomae* may be traced indirectly to the saying about the serpent in Ecclesiastes. This would have suggested parallels, including the bursting of the dragon in Bel and the Dragon (ver. 27 διερράγη); and

---

* The sense required being *stood up*, the original may have been יעמד, for which the Septuagint has ἀνιστάναι, διαμένειν, μένειν (E. A. A.).

a selection of materials would then have been made from the group of passages thus brought together.

So the *stone* in Logion V would have suggested other sayings about stones, from which a story might have been made up, with or without direct use of the Logion itself. But this was wanted to connect the raising of the stone, in some sense of the words, with the presence of Jesus.

5.

In *Evang. Thomae*, A. xviii, there is the story (Tisch. p. 155 sq.):—

Μετὰ δὲ χρόνον τινὰ οἰκοδομῆς γενομένης καὶ θορύβου μεγάλου*, ἵστατο ὁ Ἰησοῦς καὶ ἀπῆλθεν ἕως ἐκεῖ. καὶ ἰδὼν ἄνθρωπον νεκρὸν κείμενον ἐπελάβετο τῆς χειρὸς αὐτοῦ καὶ εἶπεν· σοὶ λέγω, ἄνθρωπε, ἀνάστα, ποίει τὸ ἔργον σου. καὶ εὐθέως ἀναστὰς προσεκύνησεν αὐτόν.

There is building, and a great tumult. Jesus appears *there*, sees a man lying dead, and raises him to life, saying, 'To thee I say, O man, arise: *do thy work.*'

His work was presumably building work, and therefore of the nature of that spoken of in the Logion taken literally, 'Raise the stone, cleave the wood.' The last clause of the Logion might accordingly be paraphrased,

Do thy work, and I will be with thee.

In the last chapter of *Evang. Thomae*, B (p. 89), Jesus says to Joseph 'the carpenter,'

ποίει ἀκωλύτως τὸ ἔργον σου,
Do thy work without hindrance.

6.

Logion VI, οὐδὲ ἰατρὸς ποιεῖ θεραπείας, *neither doeth a physician healings*.

The phrase ποιεῖν θεραπείας is found again in a reading of

---

* Hermas, *Sim.* ix. 3. 1, ἦν δὲ θόρυβος ... μέγας τῶν ἐληλυθότων οἰκοδομεῖν. When the stones have been raised up, the colossal man, the 'Lord of the whole tower' (ix. 6, 7), visits the structure.

Parallels to Logia

a passage of *Protevangelium Jacobi*, as we shall point out after noticing some things in the previous narrative.

Chapter xvi (Tisch. p. 30 sq.): Καὶ εἶπεν ὁ ἱερεύς· ἀπόδος τὴν παρθένον ἣν παρέλαβες ἐκ ναοῦ κυρίου. καὶ περίδακρυς ἐγένετο Ἰωσήφ. καὶ εἶπεν ὁ ἱερεύς· ποτιῶ ὑμᾶς τὸ ὕδωρ τῆς ἐλέγξεως κυρίου, καὶ φανερώσει τὰ ἁμαρτήματα ὑμῶν ἐν ὀφθαλμοῖς ὑμῶν. καὶ λαβὼν ὁ ἱερεὺς ἐπότισεν τὸν Ἰωσήφ, καὶ ἔπεμψεν αὐτὸν εἰς τὴν ὀρεινήν· καὶ ἦλθεν ὁλόκληρος. ἐπότισεν δὲ καὶ τὴν Μαριάμ, καὶ ἔπεμψεν αὐτὴν εἰς τὴν ὀρεινήν· καὶ ἦλθεν ὁλόκληρος. καὶ ἐθαύμασεν πᾶς ὁ λαὸς ὅτι ἁμαρτία οὐκ ἐφάνη ἐν αὐτοῖς. καὶ εἶπεν ὁ ἱερεύς· εἰ κύριος ὁ θεὸς οὐκ ἐφανέρωσε τὰ ἁμαρτήματα ὑμῶν, οὐδὲ ἐγὼ κρίνω ὑμᾶς.

Here we have a story about Joseph and the mother of our Lord made up from Num. v. 24, 'And he shall cause the woman to drink the water of bitterness (LXX τοῦ ἐλεγμοῦ) that causeth the curse,' and the pericope of the Woman taken in Adultery. On the birth of Jesus, the priest causes Joseph, and then Mary, to drink the water τῆς ἐλέγξεως, and when nothing happens to either, the priest says, 'If the Lord God hath not manifested your sins, neither do I *judge* you.' The *Protevangelium* has the various readings κατακρίνω, κρινῶ, found in St. John viii. 11, 'Neither do I condemn thee.'

Salome, at the end of *Protevang.* xix, expresses her doubt in the form of a parody on words of St. Thomas in the Fourth Gospel; and in the next chapter, having suffered the penalty of her unbelief, she says (Tisch. p. 38): 'Make me not an example (Matt. i. 19) to the sons of Israel, but restore me to the poor; for Thou, Lord, knowest that in Thy name I performed (v. l. ἐποίουν) τὰς θεραπείας μου.'

Thus the phrase ποιεῖν θεραπείας is found in a reading of the *Protevangelium,*

ΤΑΣ ΘΕΡΑΠΕΙΑΣ ΜΟΥ ΕΠΟΙΟΥΝ.

Compare in *Acta Pilati*, B. i (Tisch. p. 288): εἰ καλῶς ἐνήργει ΤΑΣ ΙΑΤΡΕΙΑΣ, μικρὸν ἂν ἦν τὸ κακόν· μαγείαις δὲ χρώμενος ΠΟΙΕΙ ταύτας.

III

ADDITIONAL NOTES

1.

Joseph the Carpenter.

'And when He had reached the eighth year of His age, Joseph was ordered by a certain rich man to construct a bedstead for him, for he was a carpenter.' See *Evang. Thomae*, B. xi (p. 89), comparing in Canonical Gospels, 'Is not this the carpenter's son?' (Matt. xiii. 55), 'Is not this the carpenter?' (Mark vi. 3).

The story of the bedstead according to *Evang. Thomae* A. xiii (Tisch. p. 152) begins with the statement that Joseph was a carpenter, and *made ploughs and yokes*. In Justin's *Trypho*, as quoted above (p. 53), it is said that Jesus Himself made ploughs and yokes. Pseudo-Thomas, presumably playing upon the same tradition, first makes Joseph the subject of it, and then represents Jesus as miraculously taking part in the works of Joseph.

For the bed is shorter than that a man can stretch himself on it (Isa. xxviii. 20). The miracle of the bedstead, like other curiosities of the Gospels of the Infancy, may be thought not to have been created out of nothing. Supposing pseudo-Thomas to have used Prov. xxx. 4, 'Who hath bound the waters in his garment?' (p. 95), Dr. Cotterill goes on to suggest that the next clause, 'Who hath established (LXX ἐκράτησε) all the ends of the earth?', gave rise to the story in question, in which it is said, 'Then also Jesus κρατήσας τὸ ἕτερον ἄκρον κ.τ.λ.' (B. xi. Tisch. p. 162): He takes hold of the other end, and makes the two pieces of wood equal in length.

This alone is scarcely a sufficient basis for the narrative. But Isaiah's קָצַר כִּי, 'the bed *is too short*' (Sym. & Theodot. ἐκολοβώθη) may have given the first hint of a bedstead of which a part was too short (κολοβώτερον), and an expression may then have been borrowed from the verse Prov. xxx. 4, which the writer had in mind.

It is, however, possible, as I see on further consideration of the verse, that Prov. xxx. 4 itself in the Hebrew suggested ἄκρα κραβάττου. For אֶרֶץ, *earth*, may be written ARES; and St. Jerome, as quoted in Field's *Hexapla*, writes on ערס, *bed*, in Amos iii. 12, 'sed pro hoc verbo ARES, quod Aq. interpretatus est *grabatum* . . .'. Isaiah xxviii. 20 might then have suggested that a limb of the bedstead was κολοβώτερον. The word for *bedstead* is associated in the New Testament with miracles of healing.

2.

The Gospel of pseudo-Matthew.

Pseudo-Matthew relates (cap. xx, Tisch. p. 87) that the mother of our Lord on the third day of the journey to Egypt, as she sat heated and tired under a palm-tree in the wilderness, looked up and longed to partake of its fruits. Joseph expostulates, explaining that on account of the great height of the tree this was not to be thought of. Thereupon the infant Jesus commands the tree to bow down and refresh His mother with its fruits. And forthwith at His word *inclinavit palma cacumen suum usque ad plantas Mariae*, the tree bent down its top to her feet. When they had gathered all its fruits, it remained bent down (*inclinata*), waiting for the command to rise up again (*ut resurgeret*); and when Jesus speaks the word, *statim erecta est palma*: it erects itself, and most clear, cool, sweet waters, begin to flow out through its roots.

Compare in *Epist. Barn.* xii. 1, 'Likewise again He giveth intimation concerning the cross in another prophet, saying, *And when shall these things be accomplished?* saith the Lord. *When a tree is bent down and rises again, and when blood shall drop out of a tree.*'

The Greek and the Latin of the first part of this apocryphal saying are Ὅταν ξύλον κλιθῇ καὶ ἀναστῇ, and, 'Cum lignum inclinatum fuerit et resurrexerit.' Pseudo-

Matthew's story of the palm-tree may have been founded upon this. The story is told also of a cherry-tree 'in the garden gay,' in a carol quoted by Mr. B. Harris Cowper (*Apocryphal Gospels*) 'from a chap-book printed in or about 1843 at Birmingham.'

3.
The Gospel of Peter.

(1) In the Akhmîm Fragment of the *Gospel of Peter* the cross at the Resurrection comes up from the underworld. The words in *Epist. Barn.* xii, ὅταν ξύλον ... ἀναστῇ, which mean there, when the cross shall rise up again, may have been known to pseudo-Peter, and would have suggested his resurrection of the cross. See also Resch, *Paralleltexte zu den Evangelien*, Matt. xxviii. 2–4.

(2) The cross on its resurrection is asked, Didst thou preach to them that sleep?, and utters the response, 'Yea.' This was ὁ λόγος ὁ τοῦ σταυροῦ, the *word* of the cross (1 Cor. i. 18). So the Midrash proves from the 'word' of the frogs in the Hebrew of Exod. viii. 12 that 'the frogs spoke.'

(3) In the writer's art. 3 on the *Gospel of Peter* in the *Guardian* (Feb. 7, 1894) it was suggested that 'Peter' alludes to the maltreatment of the scapegoat, which in *Epist. Barn.* vii. and elsewhere is assumed to have been enjoined and practised: 'Give heed how the type of Jesus is made manifest. *And spit ye all upon it, and pierce it*, ... and so let it be cast into the wilderness.' According to the Mishnah (*Yoma*, vi. 4), the Babylonians plucked its hair, but the Gemara explains 'Babylonians' by *Alexandrines*. Perhaps the Egyptian Gospel suggested pseudo-Peter's σύρωμεν κ.τ.λ.

4.
The Egyptian Gospel.

The last things will be *as the first* (p. 72) when *the two shall be one* (p. 70). The proposed derivation of the saying
ΕϹΤΑΙ ΤΑ ΔΥΟ ΕΝ

Additional Notes 103

from Genesis is confirmed by other words in the replies of the Lord to Salome according to the Gospel κατ' Αἰγυπτίους (p. 49),

τῇ Σαλώμῃ πυνθανομένῃ, μέχρι πότε θάνατος ἰσχύσει, εἶπεν ὁ κύριος· Μέχρις ἂν ὑμεῖς αἱ γυναῖκες τίκτετε ... Πᾶσαν φάγε βοτάνην, τὴν δὲ πικρίαν ἔχουσαν μὴ φάγῃς ... Ὅταν οὖν τὸ τῆς αἰσχύνης ἔνδυμα πατήσητε, καὶ ὅταν γένηται τὰ δύο ἕν, καὶ τὸ ἄρρεν μετὰ τῆς θηλείας, οὔτε ἄρρεν οὔτε θῆλυ.

Turning to the Old Testament for an answer to the question about death, we find there the explanation of the form of these mysterious sayings to Salome, namely in the verses of Genesis ii–iii:

ii. [21] And the Lord God caused a deep sleep to fall upon the man, and he slept; and he took one of his ribs ... [22] and the rib, which the Lord God had taken from the man, builded he into a woman, and he brought her unto the man ... [24] Therefore shall a man leave his father and his mother and cleave unto his wife: and they (LXX *the two*) shall be one flesh. [25] And they were both (LXX *the two*) naked, the man and his wife, and they were not ashamed.

iii. [1] Now the serpent was more subtil than every beast of the field ... And he said unto the woman, Yea, hath God said, Ye shall not eat of every tree of the garden? [2] And the woman said unto the serpent, Of the fruit of the trees of the garden we may eat: [3] but of the fruit of the tree which is in the midst of the garden, God hath said, Ye shall not eat of it, neither shall ye touch it, lest ye die. [6] And ... she took of the fruit thereof, and did eat; and she gave also unto her husband with her, and he did eat. [7] And the eyes of them both (LXX *the two*) were opened, and they knew that they were naked; and they sewed fig leaves together, and made themselves aprons ... [16] Unto the woman he said, ... in sorrow thou shalt bring forth children ... [17] And unto Adam he said, ... [18] thou shalt eat the herb of the field; [19] in the sweat of thy face shalt thou eat bread, till thou return unto the ground; for ... dust thou art, and unto dust shalt thou return ... [21] And the Lord God made for Adam and for his wife coats of skins, and clothed (ἐνέδυσεν) them.

μέχρι πότε θάνατος ;] The reply is, Death shall prevail as long as *ye women bring forth*, because 'unto the woman he said τέξῃ, *thou shalt bring forth*, and to Adam, ... *unto dust shalt thou return*.' Death and birth are set over against one another: the one will go on as long as the other. In the world to come there will be no death and no increasing and multiplying (Matt. xxii. 30, Rev. xxi. 4, *Jewish Fathers*, iii. n. 40).

πᾶσαν φάγε βοτάνην] *Eat every herb, but that which hath bitterness eat not.* Adam and Eve might eat of every tree but one, 'the tree of the knowledge of good and evil.' Cf. 'and thou shalt eat the herb (χόρτον) of the field.'

τὴν δὲ πικρίαν ἔχουσαν] Compare Eccles. i. 18 ὁ προστιθεὶς γνῶσιν προσθήσει ἄλγημα. Wisdom viii. 16 οὐ γὰρ ἔχει πικρίαν ἡ συναναστροφὴ αὐτῆς.

τὸ τῆς αἰσχύνης ἔνδυμα] When ye trample *the clothing of shame.* Adam and Eve were at first 'naked and not ashamed.' Afterwards they were ashamed (iii. 7 sq.), and God *clothed* them.

τὰ δύο ἕν] *When the two become one* again*, not male, not female, but male and female in one (p. 70): man the right side and woman the left (*Jewish Fathers*, ii. n. 17). Thus the doctrine of *right* and *left* comes under the same category as 'The two shall be one.'

If mystical sayings to Salome based on words of Genesis were in the Egyptian Gospel, it may have comprised other such adaptations from the ancient Scriptures. Thus it may have contained (1) the substance of what Barnabas has to say on the ceremonies of the Day of Atonement: (2) Logion II, derived from words of the Law and the Prophets relating to that Day: and (3) Logion III, a

---

* With the Preacher's, '*two together are better than one alone*,' compare, 'It is not good that the man should be alone.'

variation upon words of or concerning Wisdom in the Old Testament (p. 81) and the Apocrypha. The same Gospel may have included Logion VIII, if this was an application of the doctrine of right and left (p. 65).

Lastly, if the Gospel of Thomas shows traces of one or more of the Oxyrhynchus Logia, and if these are excerpts from the Egyptian Gospel, we are thus brought to the not unreasonable conclusion, that the eclectic author of a later Gospel romance had recourse for some of his multifarious materials to the then famous Gospel according to the Egyptians.

THE END.

OXFORD
PRINTED AT THE CLARENDON PRESS
BY HORACE HART, M.A.
PRINTER TO THE UNIVERSITY

www.ingramcontent.com/pod-product-compliance
Lightning Source LLC
Chambersburg PA
CBHW020142170426
43199CB00010B/857